Uncommon Sense

A View From The Middle

John Roberts

SEA SPARROW PRODUCTIONS

EDISTO ISLAND, SOUTH CAROLINA, U.S.A.

ISBN 978-0-9907964-0-4

Printed in the United States of America

PUBLISHER'S NOTE

Introduction

As originally conceived and initially drafted, I was going to title this book "Common Sense" – a title taken from the famous Revolutionary War-era pamphlet written by Thomas Paine, in which he argued that America should cast off British rule and declare its independence.

But then I learned that others had pre-empted my modern use of that title to justify their dissatisfaction with our government. So I tried different titles, none really satisfactory.

One day, however, I saw the following words posted on the signboard of a Howard Johnson's Inn while driving into Aiken, South Carolina: "Common sense has become so scarce that it is now uncommon."

And I had my title: *Uncommon Sense – A View from the Middle.*

With the increased polarization of American politics over the past 50-plus years, it seems to this rather ordinary American citizen that someone needs to introduce a new measure of common sense into our political thought and practices, a common sense that reflects the times in which we live and a view from the political mid-ground rather than from the ideological left or right.

Moreover, insofar as our political and media leaders have been unable to bring even the smallest measure of common sense to our political dialogue, the task is obviously left to ordinary citizens. And therein lies my purpose in writing this book: To begin that task.

First, let me suggest that using Paine's words today to justify any political viewpoint takes those words out of their historical context. Consider the following: In 1776, Paine believed British rule of the 13 colonies had become oppressive and wrote his *Common Sense* urging the colonies to declare their independence *while they were small enough to be united in their goals.*

More than two centuries later, I am writing my *Uncommon Sense* with the hope of encouraging a stronger and more effective union at a time when the nation that evolved from those original 13 colonies has grown into an extraordinarily large, diverse, complex and polarized society that, on the political surface, is anything but united in its goals.

At the most basic level, Paine was dealing with only one issue in 1776 – the question of independence from British rule. In the 21st century, we are dealing with a variety of issues reflecting the greatly increased complexity of our time. And, for that reason, I am writing not just one pamphlet as did Paine, but a series of "pamphlets" – or chapters – in a book.

I'm doing this because I believe the divisive forces at work in these United States of America seriously threaten the stability and unity of our country. Those forces – political in their expression – are a direct result of enormous growth in our population, its diversity and the rapidly increasing complexity of our lives, technology and the world in which we live. The most obvious impact of these forces has been the dramatic changes in our lives, our society, our politics, and our government.

Think about it. The first 100 years of our nation's existence saw the transition of basic transportation in the United State from the human foot, horse and wagon, and sailing ships at the time of our Declaration of Independence to the development first of steamships and then of railroads. It took only another 30 years or so for horseless carriages (automobiles) to begin replacing the horse and buggy for local travel. In 1903, at the same time the early automobiles were beginning to make inroads, the Wright brothers made their first successful airplane flight. Less than 30 years later, airplanes were crossing oceans. In another 30-odd years, men were orbiting the earth. And, in 1969, men took the first steps on the surface of the moon. Today, air travel and space flight are treated by the public as routine.

Even more dramatic....In just 35 years or so since the first personal computers were introduced, they have become ubiquitous. In roughly the past 10 years, cell phones have gone from exceptional to commonplace. We now have cell phones and computers combined into the same handheld device. Twitter. Facebook. YouTube. I hesitate to compile this short list because it will be outdated before I finish writing. But the point is obvious: Change is happening rapidly and it is accelerating. Moreover, these examples are only of changes in technology.

Think about the changes since 1776 in our national geography. And in our population.

In 1776, the 13 colonies all extended down the East Coast. Today, the 50 states extend north to Alaska and west to Hawaii. Puerto Rico and the U.S. Virgin Islands lie in the northern Caribbean, while Guam and American Samoa are thousands of miles west of Hawaii – all part of the United States of America.

In 1776, the population of the 13 original colonies was an estimated 2.5 million. By 1800, it had more than doubled to some 5.3 million. By the turn of the next century, as the result of a combination of immigration and the importation of African slaves, the country's population had reached just over 76 million. Today, our population has ballooned to more than 300 million. And that number continues to grow.

Moreover, we have grown from a country in 1776 composed mainly of white British and European immigrants to a nation whose diverse population can trace its family origins to almost every country in the world.

Today, white Americans (non-Hispanic) represent about 64 percent of our population; Hispanic Americans, about 16 percent; African Americans, 13.5 percent; and Asian Americans, about 5 percent. By 2050, according to Census Bureau estimates, non-Hispanic whites will account for less than 47 percent of the population. In other words, they will be a minority!

In 1776, most churches in the fledgling country were of various Protestant Christian denominations. Communities were small. Most schools were one-room local schools and everyone in the community knew all of the students. Even "cities" were small. Boston, New York and Charleston each had populations of only about 5,000 in 1776. Philadelphia, where the founding fathers met to write and sign the Declaration of Independence, was the largest city in the colonies with an estimated population of 25,000. My goodness, we have churches today in the United States with congregations larger than that!

What all of these changes mean is that we live in a vastly different country from the mostly rural, homogenous society of our nation's founders.

For some people, these changes are threatening – alarming even. For others, the changes are welcome. And the political struggles of the past 50 years echo those differing viewpoints.

Unfortunately, too few of the people involved in this struggle have stopped to think about the implications of these changes for our country. Instead, they have been driven on the left and on the right by political beliefs forged in an earlier era – beliefs often held as firmly as if they were religious beliefs. And, like religious beliefs, they are not open to challenge.

There is, however, one major problem with this state of affairs. And that is this: Eventually, political beliefs must bump into reality.

Our nation is confronted today by serious challenges and problems. Those challenges and problems require – no, they *demand* – solutions responsive to the world we live in today rather than to ideas or ideals that were responsive to the world 200, 100 or, even, 50 years ago. These challenges and problems demand common-sense 21st century solutions – solutions that are pragmatic in nature, solutions that are consistent with the ideals on which this nation was founded, and solutions that will actually solve the problems and effectively meet the challenges they are intended to address.

Of course, attempting to rally people behind the politics of common sense will not be easy. For one thing, common sense requires thought. (That's why it is so uncommon!) For another, it requires an open mind. That is, it requires a mind that is open to the possibility that long-held political beliefs may no longer be valid. Common sense also requires the ability to adapt one's thinking to changing circumstances.

I do not expect everyone to agree with everything I have to say. Or even, necessarily, with most of what I have to say. But I hope that everyone who takes the time to read these ideas will do more than merely react to them, more than merely accept or reject them. Or, worse yet, simply attack them.

Instead, if you think something is wrong with my ideas, make them better. If you don't like them at all, offer constructive alternatives. We shouldn't be debating simply to win an argument. We should be problem-solving together. Because it is only by mobilizing the brainpower of *thinking* Americans that we can develop ideas and programs and regulations and policies that can move this nation forward as a unified whole. Otherwise, we will simply sink lower and lower into the existing cesspool of partisan bickering. And that will get us nowhere good.

One final note: While I have addressed a number of specific subjects in the various chapters, only a few of those subjects can be considered in isolation. Most are interrelated. For example, if we are unable to address the issues raised in the first four chapters, the likelihood of bringing about any worthwhile change in the issues addressed in subsequent chapters is almost certainly zero.

One more thing: I would ask that you pick up this book with an open mind – that is, a mind open to hearing and giving serious consideration to ideas that might be different from your own. If you cannot do that, you might as well put the book down.

Now, let's begin the journey.

Table of Contents

Part I: Government and Society

Chapter 1: The United States: A Three-legged Stool 1

The author uses the analogy of a three-legged stool to illustrate the importance of maintaining equilibrium among the three pillars of our social foundation: Society (the people), government and business. As long as the three are in equilibrium, the nation (the stool) is stable. If, however, one of those legs becomes more powerful (longer) than the others, stability is threatened. Today, he argues, the stability of our system is threatened and he points us in directions for regaining the needed equilibrium among these three structural components of our political-socio-economic system.

Chapter 2: An Independent Congress – Part I 5

The founders of our American democracy intended to create a government of three co-equal and independent branches – the Executive, Legislative and Judicial. But they were thinking only of the relationship of the three branches to each other. They did not foresee the practice of politics as it exists today, or that the Legislative branch might someday be sold to the highest bidder — effectively the situation in which we find ourselves today. In this chapter, the author lays out three steps for taking Congress back from the powerful interest groups that now control it so that we can once again have a truly "independent" Congress.

The January 2010 U.S. Supreme Court decision related to corporations and political speech coalesced long-held questions in the author's mind about the increasing legal personification of corporations in America. This chapter discusses some of the implications of that decision, calls into question the justification by Justice Kennedy of the extension of First Amendment rights to corporations as "associations of citizens," and wonders whether our founding fathers, if they had foreseen the emergence of corporations in America, would have started the Preamble to the U. S. Constitution with the following words: "We the flesh and blood people of the United States of America…."

One of the ongoing areas of argument among different political groups is the question of how much is too much when it comes to government. In this chapter, the author points to changes that have taken place over the past two centuries in the social and economic complexities and the realities in which Americans live and argues that the question should not be "how much" but instead, "what roles should government fill" in this, the 21st century.

Part II: Specific Issues

The author begins this chapter by reproducing the Preamble to the U.S. Constitution, then posits that the dramatically increased concentration of the nation's wealth into the hands of a small portion of the population over the past 25 or more years threatens to disrupt our "more perfect union" by undermining "domestic tranquility" and the "general welfare," thereby potentially toppling our three-legged societal stool. Insofar as past changes in personal and corporate income tax laws have redistributed the nation's wealth by funneling it increasingly into the hands of the wealthy, the solution to this emerging crisis, he suggests, requires reversing those changes and a serious tightening of corporate tax laws so that our corporations as well as our wealthier citizens provide a significantly larger share of the nation's tax revenue.

Taxes are one of the most contentious issues in our society. Unfortunately, in a society in which private citizens own the means for creating wealth, taxes are the only means available to government to finance its operations. The question, therefore, the author argues, is not whether there should be taxes, but how they should be structured. In the balance of this chapter, he offers a common-sense approach to discussion of taxes and several provocative suggestions for changes in the structure of our tax system, including the use of special-purpose taxes to influence corporate behavior.

Chapter 7: America's New Indentured Servants 69

In the 30 years since tiny Delaware liberalized its usury laws to entice major credit card banks to the state by effectively allowing them free rein to run their businesses, tens of millions of Americans have, in effect, become indentured servants to the credit card banks. This chapter explains how this situation came about, how the banks have "justified" their actions, and offers suggestions for curbing the banks' power over their indentured servants – power which, despite changes in federal law governing credit card operations, remains effectively undiminished.

Chapter 8: The War on Drugs 85

America's 30-year "War on Drugs" has been an unmitigated failure. In this chapter, the author explains why, despite many billions of tax dollars spent in this unrelenting campaign against illegal drugs, the "war" has failed, why it can never be won by continuing the same policies, and then explains in detail how a common sense alternative would bring an end to the drug cartels' stranglehold on America.

Chapter 9: Energy – Part I 95

In this chapter, the author suggests that our political leaders are following fads in their efforts to reduce our oil consumption and ignoring simple, common-sense steps that would quickly and dramatically cut our use of petroleum fuels. But he does not generalize. He offers specific common-sense suggestions, some of which might not – probably would not – be popular at the outset, but would be immediately effective. He also offers additional suggestions that would take longer to implement, but would also be equally cost-effective.

In this chapter, the author looks at a different side of the energy equation – our consumption of electricity now generated principally by burning coal, oil or natural gas. Again, he offers common-sense suggestions for reducing our consumption of electricity, not the least of which is the importance of taking the Law of Unintended Consequences into consideration when making significant changes – for example, the use of compact fluorescent light bulbs to replace incandescent bulbs.

The growth of partisanship over the past 50 years, the author writes here, has reached the point at which, for too many people, political party and ideology apparently have become more important than country. He argues that reliance on ideology (which often blinds its believers to reality), the adoption of propaganda techniques by political operatives to win public opinion, and the intimidation and failure of news media to serve its watchdog function have combined to bring about this situation. While he offers no magic bullet to bring an end to partisanship, the author does provide several common-sense suggestions to the news media of ways they can regain their role as the guardian of democracy.

Chapter 12: Prescription Drugs in the United States of America 137

Americans pay what are arguably the highest prices in the world for prescription drugs while patients in other countries often pay only pennies on the dollar for the same drug products. In this chapter, the author uses facts and common sense to call into question the pharmaceutical industry's claim that it needs to charge Americans those high prices to support its search for new and more effective drug products and to achieve the high earnings needed to attract investors to the industry. He then suggests actions an independent Congress could take to curb some of the industry's excesses and, in all probability, bring down the cost of drugs for the American consumer.

Chapter 13: The Politics of Climate Change 143

In this chapter, the author offers a common-sense way of looking at the issue of climate change and deciding what to do about it by asking two simple questions: (1) What would be the consequence of assuming predictions of global warming are valid, taking actions to reduce its effects, and discovering 20 or 30 years later that the theory was baloney? And (2), what would be the consequences of assuming the theory is baloney, taking no action, and discovering 20 or 30 years in the future that we were wrong – that the theory was correct?

Chapter 14: Getting Things Done in Congress – The KISS Strategy 163

The debates in Congress in recent years over health care and the national budget have shown clearly the difficulty of attempting to gain Congressional approval of major pieces of legislation. In this chapter, the author suggests a new way for political leaders to get important legislation through Congress. It is the KISS strategy – as in, Keep It Simple Stupid!

There is widespread agreement that our public schools are failing many of our students. The author argues in this chapter that our traditional view of education and our failure to recognize the importance of the family component in education make it impossible for our schools to the meet the needs of a large portion of today's children. He offers specific common sense suggestions for changes in the administration of our schools, changes in the middle and upper school curricula, and changes in the relationship between schools and parents that he believes will enable our public schools to fulfill their role much more effectively.

Here the author asks and then discusses a critical but profoundly simple question: If one starts with the belief that there is a God, and that God is indeed the Creator, how do we reconcile a God who would create such diversity in the world – diversity of minerals and rocks, of elements, and of plant and animal life; diversity of weather, of environments and ecosystems; and diversity among humans in their skin colors, their facial bone structures, their eye shapes and colors, their languages, their cultures and their beliefs – how do we reconcile that God, the Creator of such diversity, with the notion of a God who would tolerate only one faith and only one way of acknowledging Him and worshipping Him?

Chapter 17: Firearms in the United States of America 197

This chapter begins with the Second Amendment to the Constitution. The author goes on to argue that the amendment was not intended as a blanket guarantee of the right of citizens to own guns as is generally argued today, but was instead expressly intended to provide for state militias to serve as an alternative to a large, standing army. Those militias today are found in the person of the various National Guard units. It is time, he argues, for the courts to recognize this historical fact and to stop impeding government efforts to restrict gun ownership.

Chapter 18: Final Thoughts 205

In this last chapter, the author has assembled additional observations related to the following: (1) Congress as a career; (2) the news media; (3) income taxes and (4) our country at a crossroads.

The United States: A Three-Legged Stool

1

The framers of our Constitution lived in a much less complex world. They were not concerned about economics or an economic system. Their concerns involved the rights and freedom of individuals. They envisioned a system in which government served the people, as opposed to a system like the one they left behind in England in which the people served government.

Indeed, they constructed their new nation on a foundation of two pillars: one pillar was "We the People;" the second pillar was "government." Moreover, they very consciously structured the system so those two entities would keep each other in balance. The people had certain constitutional rights and the power of the ballot box. Government had the role of maintaining order, protecting the public welfare and protecting the rights of the people. Going a step further, they designed a government of three parts – Executive, Legislative and Judicial — each with powers that provided a system of checks and balances within the government itself to help ensure that government did not overstep.

Our founding fathers, however, did not foresee — and could not have foreseen — the evolution of our modern economic system and the role of capitalism (business) in our country today. Nor could they have foreseen the complex political and socio-economic system that effectively defines our country today as a result – a socio-economic system that also can be described as a three-legged stool.

The legs of that stool are government, society (the public) and capitalism (the business community). As long as all three legs are of equal length, the stool – i.e., the country – is stable. If one leg becomes longer (stronger) and/or another leg becomes shorter (weaker), the stool becomes unstable.

Among this trio, I see capitalism as the driving force of our business system, society as the beneficiary of that system, and government as the moderator between the sometimes conflicting interests of the other two. I also see capitalism as the primary source of instability in our socioeconomic system. When – not if, but when – business becomes too powerful and society begins to be short-changed, the stool (our overall socio-economic system) becomes unstable.

This instability arises because of the basic nature of capitalism: The only purpose of capitalism is to make profits. You can say whatever you want to say about building companies, advancing technology, or whatever, but those are merely the means by which the capitalist makes profits. In fact, the modern corporation has only one goal – that is, to make money for its shareholders.

That is not good or bad. It's just reality. Things such as "serving the public interest" or "being a good corporate citizen" are simply necessary tactics in the corporate pursuit of profits. And anyone who thinks differently is being naïve.

Capitalism – our system of business in the United States – is without question the most dynamic and rewarding economic system the world knows. By providing incentive, it stimulates invention and hard work. By providing rewards, it encourages investment and economic risk-taking. Because it operates with the goal of profit, it is generally efficient. And by providing jobs, it has the means to bring about broad prosperity.

But capitalism also has its dangers – dangers most likely to arise when capitalism is taken to extremes. When this happens, usually it is society that suffers the negative consequences and, as a result, the stool becomes unstable. Government too may suffer if corporations and the people who run them become so powerful that they can influence government to their own selfish ends (i.e. more profit), making the stool even more unstable (see Chapter 2 – An Independent Congress).

We've seen this instability occur off and on in two areas over the past 150 years or so. The first business excesses that come to mind brought about the growth of labor unions, beginning in the mid-1800s with ups and downs and both turbulent and less turbulent times throughout the years. Government finally stepped in with the passage of the National Labor Relations Act in 1935 to bring a measure of stability into the previously volatile conflict between workers and employers.

Additional laws establishing such things as a minimum wage, a 40-hour work week, overtime pay, anti-discrimination laws, and regulations intended to ensure a safe working environment have also been enacted to provide a counterbalance to the power of business in dealing with its employees.

A second cause of instability in our three-legged stool involved the growth of corporate monopolies in some industries. This resulted in passage of the Sherman Antitrust Act in 1890 and subsequent related measures that enabled government to break up the monopolistic excesses of capitalism in the 19th and 20th centuries.

The recent financial crisis (the worst recession since the Great Depression of 1929 and the 1930s), the national debate over health care and the rapidly growing influence of corporations in our political process have made it clear that our three-legged stool has once again become unstable. And once again, government needs to restrain the excesses of capitalism to restore stability to our system.

One obvious step toward accomplishing this involves finding some means to take the money out of politics (See Chapter 2 — An Independent Congress — Part I). Another obvious step is more regulation – regulation aimed at curbing specific excesses, such as the usurious interest rates consumers are charged on credit card debt (See Chapter 7 – America's New Indentured Servants). But there are excesses – much more subtle excesses carried out in the pursuit of profit — that cannot be moderated by regulation. Some of these, however – or, at least, some of their negative effects — can be moderated through the creative use of taxation (See Chapter 6 – Taxes: Too Much or Too Little).

But the key to any such governmental restraint on the excesses of our business system is for us to regain an independent Congress.

An Independent Congress – Part I

2

In writing the Constitution of the United States of America, our founding fathers sought to provide a system of checks and balances by establishing three independent branches of government, each equally powerful – an executive branch; a legislative branch, and a judicial branch. We know these as the Office of the President, the Congress and the Supreme Court. Of course, when the framers of our Constitution thought of these as independent branches of government, they meant independent of each other.

Unfortunately, they – the "framers" – did not envision the role that money would come to play in our political processes. Or that this country would reach the point at which money would bind members of Congress so tightly to their campaign contributors it would no longer be an "independent" branch of government.

But that is, in fact, the situation we have today. Congress is not free to legislate solely on the basis of what is good for the country because every single member of the House of Representatives and the Senate is totally dependent upon campaign contributions to stay in office.

Think about it. When someone is elected to the House of Representatives, no sooner does he or she take office than it is necessary to begin raising money for the reelection campaign, which will start in just 15 or 18 months, depending upon whether there will be a primary challenger. In many cases, the fund raising process may even start before the member is sworn in.

For members of the Senate, the fund raising pressure is a little less immediate; they have five and a half years to build up their war chests. But the basic problem is the same and the pressure is equally intense. With few exceptions (e.g., Delaware and Rhode Island) Senate campaigns cost much more than those of House candidates because senators have to campaign statewide. As a result, even though they have more time to raise money, most senators need to raise a lot more of it.

The problems this situation causes have been particularly obvious in recent years. Effectively, members of Congress have become so beholden to their contributors that they often are not free to vote for what may be best for the country. They know full well that when an issue important to one or more of their campaign donors arises, they will be besieged by lobbyists who will certainly find ways to remind them (even if unspoken) how helpful the organization they represent has been to the member in his effort to raise funds for his campaign. And even though the members will never admit it, they also know deep down in their private souls that they really are not free to vote their consciences on many issues. Instead, they find "ideological" arguments to explain their votes on these issues.

Moreover, in its April 2014 decision abolishing the decades-old limit on the amount of money any individual could contribute to candidates for federal office in any two-year election cycle, the U.S. Supreme Court has made the situation even worse.

From a practical perspective, this means that every member of Congress owes allegiance to two constituencies that often have conflicting interests. The traditional constituency is composed of the public – the people who live in the member's district or state. The new constituency is made up of major campaign donors. And the overriding problem is this: With the present system of campaign finance, every member of Congress knows that he cannot be reelected without those campaign donors. As a result, when forced to choose between the interests of their major campaign-donor constituencies and the best interest of their public constituencies, too often our members of Congress vote for the interests of the organizations and people that fund their campaigns.

Voters know this, of course. They are not stupid. Why else does anyone believe that Congress is held in such low esteem by the electorate? I personally believe that most if not all members of Congress have become little more than legislative prostitutes, selling themselves to their campaign donors. And I know that I am not alone in this feeling.

I also know even as I write these words that members of Congress will take great exception to them. But I am also confident that if they will be truly honest with themselves – and that means facing an ugly truth – they will admit at least to themselves if to no one else that what I have written is often true. Maybe they won't admit it about themselves, but about some of their peers. Moreover, I don't think any of the members are happy with this situation.

First, too much time is taken courting potential donors and trying to find ways to keep donors happy – time that should be spent doing what the members know is their job. Second, getting reelected or elected in the first place has become a fund-raising contest in which the winner too often is likely to be the person with the most money to spend on the campaign.

Third, and most importantly, I truly believe that most people who seek public office do so with the noblest of intentions – that is, to serve the public interest. And no one who enters Congress with that noble intention can be happy with the constant need to be out raising campaign funds and the interlocking network of unspoken but very real obligations those fund raising activities create.

It is time to change the system – to take campaign contributions and the obligations they create out of the system; to put an end to the upward spiral in the costs of election campaigns; and, by doing those two things, to enable our representatives and senators to cast off their chains of bondage.

This is not a pipe dream. It is something that can be done. We really can regain an independent Congress – that is, a Congress whose members are freed from obligations to contributors – if we want to. We really can regain a Congress whose members are free to vote their consciences and who can go back to their constituents with pride to explain why they have voted the way they did without worrying about the possible effects of that vote on their campaign-fund-raising ability. All it requires is a bit of common sense and a lot of political courage.

Common sense suggests three interrelated steps, each reinforcing the other.

First, the House and Senate should pass legislation to provide for public funding of campaigns for all elective federal offices, not just for president and vice president. That public funding should be related to the population and geographic size of the district or state in which the candidate must run. It should also be distributed equally among opposing candidates and include a provision that, if Candidate A refuses to accept public funding for his campaign, the public funds available to Candidate B will be supplemented as necessary to match Candidate A's campaign spending.

Second, the House and Senate should enact changes in their respective ethics rules that would require a member to recuse himself from voting on legislation (except for personal income tax legislation) that would have a financial impact on anyone in his family or on any organization that gave him contributions exceeding $1,000 in the aggregate or that has sponsored or co-sponsored third party campaign spending on his behalf during the campaign for his current term of office, or in anticipation of any future campaign. This would include the aggregate of contributions from executives of any one organization. Failure to comply with this ethics provision should be grounds for censure at a minimum and expulsion from Congress at a maximum.

Third, Congress should enact legislation requiring that any organization sponsoring advertisements supporting a specific candidate or running so-called "issue" campaign ads or other publicity programs on behalf of a candidate or an issue being debated in Congress must identify publicly and prominently as part of that advertisement or publicity program, the sources of all funding. Moreover, the identification of funding should reach back to the original source of the funds and be as prominently displayed or aired as are the potential side effects in advertisements for prescription drugs.

So, for example, if a public relations agency contributes to a public interest group so that the public interest group can sponsor an advertisement or public meeting or a march on Washington supporting a candidate or one side of an issue, such an outreach effort would be required to identify not only the public interest group, but also the public relations agency and all of its clients who have paid the agency to put that message before the public.

In other words, the financial support for the political interests of a company, union or other organization could not be "laundered" by passing it through a series of public relations or advertising agencies and/or non-profit grass roots or public interest groups.

In addition, there should be severe penalties imposed for failure to comply completely with this disclosure requirement.

Some people might argue that such a proposal would interfere with the free-speech rights of the organizations affected. I disagree. Those organizations or wealthy individuals would still be perfectly free to put their viewpoints into the public domain. They would simply be unable to hide their identities behind the false front of another group. The only excuse I can think of for continuing the current laundering of campaign and political-issue financial support is that the organizations or individuals hiding their identities in this manner are afraid to be publicly identified with the viewpoints they are supporting, or their support for individual candidates.

If these three actions were taken, I believe our lawmakers would regain their independence and that public confidence in Congress would greatly improve.

The first step – enactment of public funding for campaigns – would free members from all of the fund-raising activities that now demand so much of their time. The result would be more time for them to spend on their jobs as legislators. They would actually have time to review legislation and know first-hand the details of legislation they will vote on instead of relying on summaries provided by staff or some lobbying organization. (Remember all of those complaints we hear that members often lack time to study the bill they are being asked to vote on?)

Of course, no one could be forced to accept public funding and members could choose to continue taking time from their legislative responsibilities to raise campaign funds. But imagine the campaign in which one candidate accepts public funding and refuses campaign contributions of more than $1,000 and the other candidate accepts large corporate contributions. From the beginning of that campaign, the source of campaign funds would be an issue. Which candidate do you think would have the greater credibility in voters' eyes? I may be an innocent, but I believe it would not take long for public financing to become the funding of choice for most candidates.

Of course, there's another option – one taken by Arizona, North Carolina, New Mexico and Wisconsin. Each of these states provides for public funding of some elections. In Arizona, all candidates for statewide and legislative offices can choose public funding of their election campaigns. In North Carolina, New Mexico and Wisconsin, public funding is available on a voluntary basis for both primary and general election campaigns for candidates for appellate judicial positions. In addition to providing campaign funding these laws generally provide for extra funding if spending by a candidate who has opted out of public funding for his campaign exceeds a certain amount.

But that question – whether to choose public or private campaign funding – is the reason the suggested change in ethics rules in both chambers of Congress and the identification of individuals and/or organizations paying for so-called "issue" campaign ads is so important. If members of Congress were required to recuse themselves from voting on legislation that would have direct economic impact on major contributors to their campaigns, the campaign contributions would not have the desired effect – that is, they could not influence the members' votes – and the financial contributions would dry up.

Think about it for a moment: If all members of Congress who received campaign contributions from the health insurance industry, pharmaceutical companies and hospitals, or from their various industry trade associations, had been required to recuse themselves from voting (i.e., had declared themselves ineligible to vote) on the healthcare legislation as it worked its way through Congress, we would have had an interesting situation.

This ethics rule – recusing oneself from voting on an issue in which one has a personal interest – is not a novel idea. It is standard practice among judges, who are required by their ethics rules to recuse themselves from hearing any case in which they or their family members have an interest in the outcome. Interestingly, the failure of some judges to recuse themselves when they should have is what prompted moves to public funding of campaigns for judicial offices in some states where judges are elected. This ethical requirement extends to include U.S. Supreme Court Justices. It should also extend to members of Congress.

Such an ethics rule change would go a long way toward ending corporate, labor or other single-issue organizations – for example, the Sierra Club and the National Rifle Association, etc. – from trying to win support for candidates through their financial contributions. Instead, they would be forced to rely solely on the strength of their arguments, and on their ability to openly persuade the electorate on the issue rather than on their ability to provide both direct *and* indirect financial support behind the scenes to one candidate or another.

These changes can be made if "We the People" demand them. There would, of course, be massive resistance to these ideas from the power brokers who now control Congress through their campaign contributions. They do not want to lose the leverage they enjoy among members of Congress under the present system. In fact, if Congress were to take up the proposals I've suggested, the lobbying efforts against these proposals would dwarf the efforts to oppose healthcare legislation in 2009!

All stops would be pulled. The public interest groups, unions, corporations, and trade associations would gang up like we've never seen before. They would oppose these changes with every weapon at their disposal. They would be joined in this effort to derail such change by most public relations and advertising companies and, probably, by media conglomerates. There would, of course, also be court challenges to any law requiring disclosure of third party financing of campaign activities.

Why? Because the interest groups, unions, corporations and trade associations know that reason alone will not enable them to block legislation they oppose. And, because the advertising and public relations companies and media conglomerates know that such changes will take huge bites out of their profits in every election year.

Now, let the record show that I am not against lobbying. Lobbying to me means presenting your viewpoint on legislation in as persuasive a manner as possible with the hope that your viewpoint will be taken into consideration by lawmakers regarding whatever proposal is before Congress.

Lobbying, in my opinion, is essential to good legislation. You cannot expect any member of Congress to know intuitively all of the potential ramifications of any legislation. It is critically important for legislators to hear as many different viewpoints as possible so they can make informed decisions that will help craft the best possible piece of legislation. Lobbying without money will help make that possible.

Frankly, lobbying with money makes that impossible.

One argument the various interest groups and some members of Congress will make is that taxpayers can ill afford to finance all of those campaigns. The cost is just too great.

But I have a profoundly simple, common sense question about the cost of election campaigns. Where is it written that a candidate must spend millions or tens of millions of dollars to get elected?

Although that is the situation existing today, it is a situation created by the present system – a competitive system in which the person who spends the most money has the best chance to win. A system in which public relations and advertising firms (pursuing their own self-interest) persuade candidates that these expenditures for television advertising are necessary for them to win their elections. More than any other factor, or even any other combination of factors, it is the spending competition that has driven up the cost of campaigns.

Why, for example, do we need all of those costly television advertisements? What's wrong with using the news media – all news media – to get your message out? What's wrong with visiting newsrooms for interviews, and doing live interviews with local radio and television stations, and with Internet bloggers? What's wrong with using the time now wasted on begging for campaign contributions to hold public meetings with voters? What's wrong with the way it was done before campaigns were taken over by public relations firms and advertising agencies? This is one instance in which I believe the "good old days" were better. The campaigns were certainly less expensive!

So let's get started. Let's take our Congress back from the many special interests that have tried with varying degrees of success to buy Congress for the past 40 or more years. Our nation really does need an independent legislative branch. And, if Congress is too cowardly to act, perhaps We the People can provide the needed backbone.

What do you think would happen, for example, if citizens in each of the 18 states[1] that allow petition-driven initiatives to change the state constitutions were to begin collecting signatures on petitions to provide for public funding of congressional election campaigns? If those ballot initiatives were successful, might they not encourage voters in other states to push their legislatures to follow that lead? As noted above, three states – North Carolina, New Mexico and Wisconsin – have already passed such legislation governing the election of appellate level judges and Arizona law provides public funding for all statewide and legislative campaigns. So it is possible.

If we can build momentum for such change in the states, Congress will be forced to come around – especially if we make providing for public funding on a federal level for congressional campaigns a campaign issue when members of Congress are up for reelection. It might take us a little time to get it done, but we can do it – if we want it badly enough.

---

[1] The 18 states allowing constitutional amendments via the ballot initiative process are Arizona, Arkansas, California, Colorado, Florida, Illinois, Massachusetts, Michigan, Mississippi, Missouri, Montana, Nebraska, Nevada, North Dakota, Ohio, Oklahoma, Oregon and South Dakota.

An Independent Congress – Part II

3

In January 2010, the U.S. Supreme Court dropped a bombshell by ruling that government limitations on political advertising by corporations represent an unconstitutional restriction on free speech. In writing for the majority, Justice Anthony M. Kennedy wrote: "If the First Amendment has any force, it prohibits Congress from fining or jailing citizens, *or associations of citizens* (emphasis added), for simply engaging in free speech."

On the surface, it would seem that all this decision did was to strike down a federal law limiting political advertising in the last days of presidential campaigns. But, as many have suggested, the implications are far more profound and potentially dangerous.

On a philosophical level, this decision has the effect of equating the First Amendment rights of corporations with those of individual people. I will grant that Justice Kennedy was very careful to avoid such an assertion by his choice of words, referring to corporations as "associations of citizens."

But that is how he justified this extension of First Amendment protection to corporate political speech – by describing a corporation as an "association of citizens."

But is it?

A corporation is in fact a legal artifact created by lawyers and chartered by a state for the purpose of doing business. It may be wholly-owned, in which case it is likely owned by one person or a couple, for example. It may be closely held, in which case there is only a small number of owners. It may be privately held with a larger number of owners. Or it may be publicly held, in which case it will likely have millions of owners who own stock directly in their brokerage accounts or indirectly through their mutual fund holdings or pension funds.

Additionally, a corporation consists of a second important group of people – its employees. Here too, depending upon the type of corporation, there may be only one or two employees (who may also be the owners) or many thousands of employees in the case of large companies publicly or privately held.

To call these organizations – particularly large, publicly held corporations – "associations of citizens," however, is at best a stretch.

Except for their common desire to make a profit, the stockholders of a large corporation might have and often do have few interests in common. Stockholders not only include wealthy individuals, but labor unions through their pension plans, and millions of other people through their IRAs, 401ks, and personal mutual fund holdings. Similarly, except for their common desire to enjoy continuity of employment, a corporation's employees also may have few interests in common and can be expected to represent a broad spectrum of political viewpoints.

What I'm suggesting is this: First, no publicly held corporation could possibly be considered in any real sense of the words as an "association of citizens." In fact, if you look at the millions of stockholders and the thousands of employees of any large corporation, you would almost certainly find that they represent the complete political spectrum of the country. Moreover, these "citizens" – stockholders and the broad group of employees – have virtually no influence on any corporate decision to support either candidates or issues.

So, given the diverse political interests of all of these stakeholders, and given that they have virtually no input into the decision to support a particular candidate or point of view on an issue, how can the U.S. Supreme Court be protecting the political speech of this so-called "association of citizens"? In fact, it doesn't. This Supreme Court decision protects only the corporate funding of the political speech of a few people at the apex of the corporate pyramid.

In other words, calling a corporation an "association of citizens" is a legal stretch so torturous that it would be humorous if it were not so serious.

But let's follow this acceptance of the "free speech rights" of corporations to its logical conclusions — something that the justices voting for the majority opinion in this case clearly failed to do.

First, this decision does not differentiate between types of corporations or the source of ownership. It presumably extends to all corporations legally domiciled in the United States.

Let me offer this scenario. Let's assume the government of China wants to influence U.S. trade policies. The government of China can instruct one of its exporting companies to establish a U.S. subsidiary to sell, for example, Chinese-made automobiles in the United States. This subsidiary would, in fact, be a U.S. corporation and would be eligible under this Supreme Court ruling to fund political advertising. *Moreover, under the existing system, the fact that the U.S. subsidiary of a foreign company was funding candidate campaigns or issue advertising would never be known because the source of funding for such political speech need not be revealed.*

Some might argue that existing restrictions on the use of foreign money in U.S. political campaigns would prevent such a subsidiary from sponsoring political advertising. But would it really? If the subsidiary of a foreign-based company is doing business in the United States, selling its products in this country, how can you claim that money being generated in this country would represent foreign money?

Toyota and Honda operations in the United States, for example, generate many millions of dollars in U.S.-based income and cash flow for their Japanese parent companies. None of that income is foreign money until it has been sent to Japan. As long as it stays in the United States, it could be spent to fund political advertising or rallies supporting candidates and/or political issues.

Now, expand that example to include an Iranian oil company. Or to various Russian state-owned or state-controlled companies. Or, for that matter, to any other country in which government effectively controls major industries. All of these entities have now had the door opened to them to participate in the political campaigns and debates of the United States Congress. Was that really the intent of the five justices who voted to extend the First Amendment to corporate political speech?

I suspect not. This is instead, I suggest, just one more example of what's known as The Law of Unintended Consequences – the one law that even the Supreme Court of the United States cannot overturn.

Let me continue in a different vein, in the direction I was heading when thinking about this matter even before the January 2010 decision – the legal treatment of corporations as people as far as the First Amendment is concerned.

For years, we have been moving toward the legal notion of a corporation as a "person" with the same Constitutional protections as individual people. This notion of a corporation as a person has bothered me for several reasons.

First, as mentioned earlier, a corporation is a legal artifact. A person is flesh and blood. That seems a basic and important difference.

Second, the impact of a single individual rarely extends beyond those with whom that person comes into contact either through his family, church, school or job. There are, of course, the occasional exceptional people, and those we call leaders. The impact of a corporation, however, can quite literally be felt worldwide and by millions upon millions of people.

Third, in the political arena, most flesh and blood people have limited resources. I cannot, for example, spend hundreds of thousands of dollars on political advertising to get a senator or congressman elected and, therefore, put him in my pocket.

Fourth, if a flesh and blood person violates the law in a serious way, he will go to prison. In a few cases and in some states, he might even be put to death.

If a corporation violates the law in a serious way, however, most often it suffers no serious consequences. Oh yes, one or two executives might go to jail if they are found guilty of criminal conduct. Or the corporation might pay a very large fine for breaking the law. On rare occasions, a corporation might even fail because its misdeeds were so atrocious. Enron is one example.

But the very real fact of the matter is this: Our legal system has no way to send a corporation to jail. Or to put a corporation to death. Or, even if there is a desire to press criminal charges against a corporation, our prosecutors have no appetite or, if an appetite, no multimillion dollar budgets for such prosecution. Corporations facing legal challenges, on the other hand, have almost unlimited budgets to spend in their defense.

Moreover, as we saw in 2008 and 2009, our major corporations can be deemed too large to be allowed to die or fail, or to be shut down (put in jail) for a period of years as punishment for misdeeds. Our federal government, in fact, bailed some of them out using billions of tax dollars even though their corporate misdeeds, misjudgments and mismanagement had crippled the nation's – indeed, the world's – economy and brought extreme hardship to millions of Americans.

If corporations are, in fact, subject to the same rights extended by our Constitution to flesh and blood people, they should also be subject to the same penalties as flesh and blood people if they violate our laws. Indeed, we should be able to enact legislation allowing corporations to be "put in jail" for breaking the law by putting their corporate charter on ice for a period of years and, therefore, denying them the right to do business in this country during that time.

So, for example, if a person were to commit fraud and be sentenced to 10 years in prison, a corporation found guilty of fraud would similarly be sentenced to ten years in "jail" by having its corporate charter withdrawn for 10 years.

But of course that can't happen.

In the first place, I question whether we have the criminal statutes that would be necessary to put a corporation as opposed to corporate officers on trial. (In fact, if that were to happen, I suspect that the first argument the corporate defense counsel would make is that a corporation is not a person and, therefore, not subject to criminal law.) In the second place, the social and economic consequences of withdrawing a corporation's charter for even just one or two years would likely be worse than the public consequences of the crime committed.

The problem is obvious. It is precisely because corporations are not people that they cannot truly be held accountable for their misdeeds. If a person is sentenced to prison, the impact of his imprisonment extends only to the one person and his loved ones. If a large corporation were to be imprisoned, thousands of people would lose their jobs. Investors would lose millions or even billions of dollars. State and local governments would lose large sources of tax revenue. And the impact would crash outward like a tsunami.

That is the strongest argument I can find against accepting corporations as "people" in a legal sense by extending to them the basic constitutional right of free speech. We do not have any truly effective way to hold a corporation truly responsible for its actions or to punish it for its misdeeds. Fines – our only recourse – are simply another cost of doing business as far as the corporation is concerned.

My other objection is pragmatic. The extension of the First Amendment right of free speech to corporations has enormously increased the political power of an already very powerful, but relative small group of people who have only one goal – that is, to make more profits for themselves and their stockholders. In fact, by extending the First Amendment protection of free speech to corporations and allowing them to spend unlimited amounts of money in political campaigns, the Court has unleashed a giant – probably many giants, even potentially including foreign governments whose interests may be at odds with our own national interests – a giant whose influence will far exceed that of our country's flesh and blood citizens.

Consider this: According to a report in *USA Today,* "outside political spending topped $1 billion in the presidential and congressional races in 2012 (the first elections held after this Supreme

Court decision), *more than three times what such groups spent in the previous election cycle* (emphasis added)."[2]

The problem in the short term is that I can see only one way to escape the consequences of this decision: that is, to find a way to enable the Court to reconsider its decision. For example, if the Congress could be persuaded to pass a new bill restricting corporate political spending and the president were to sign that bill into law, it would almost certainly be challenged in court. Hopefully, that challenge process would provide opportunity for the Court to reconsider its earlier decision. Alternatively, perhaps the Attorney General – recognizing how this court decision has opened our political process to powerful foreign influence — could find grounds to ask the court to reconsider its 2010 decision. If either of these paths can be taken, it is to be hoped that some of the justices who joined in the 2010 decision could be persuaded to rethink that decision.

In the longer term, we can do something to neutralize the effect of this decision on our political landscape by following the suggestion contained in Chapter 2, "An Independent Congress – Part I." That is, we can take money out of politics by providing public funding for *all* federal elections and by changing ethics rules to require members of Congress to follow the judicial system's precedent of recusing themselves from voting on any legislation that would benefit any person or organization that has contributed more than $1,000 to their election campaigns, *including indirect support received from third-party-funded political advertising on the member's behalf.*

As noted earlier, it is possible to make this change, but it will almost certainly have to be done one step at a time, state by state

---

[2] USA Today, February 26, 2014 – Page 2A "Outside money can change election's course"

until the moral momentum becomes so great that Congress will be forced to act. For the present, far too many members of Congress have already sold themselves to the current system for me to think that Congress will bring about these reforms on its own initiative. We the People – the flesh and blood people – will have to make them do it.

One other thought:

I sometimes wonder whether the delegates to our Constitutional Convention in 1787 would have begun the Preamble to the Constitution differently had they been able to look forward 223 years and foresee the extension of Constitutional protections to a legal artifact called a "corporation." Would they have begun our Constitution by writing, "We the *flesh and blood* people of the United States…."?

Somehow that doesn't have quite the same ring to it. But neither does, "We the people and the corporations of the United States…"

Or, if he could have foreseen the direction taken by the Supreme Court some 147 years later, would Abraham Lincoln in his Gettysburg Address have spoken of the bloody sacrifice made on that battlefield so "that the government of the people and corporations, by the people and corporations, and for the people and corporations shall not perish from this earth?"

Somehow, I think not.

The Roles of Government 4

I am repeatedly given pause by those who argue that our federal government is too big. Or that government is too intrusive. Or even those who argue for a "strict" interpretation of our Constitution by the Supreme Court. And I wonder whether people who voice these views have ever stopped to think seriously about the role of government and what it should be. For example, have those people considered the possibility that changes in our society and the emergence of the many non-governmental institutions that comprise the underlying fabric of our social and economic system have required changes in the size and role of government compared to the time when our nation was founded?

Clearly the framers of our Constitution could not have visualized a federal government as large and as broadly involved in the everyday life of the nation as is our government today. Theirs was a relatively simple nation, a largely agrarian society combined with a growing merchant trade in the coastal cities. The nation's population in 1789 when the U.S. Constitution was ratified was less than 4 million and 95 percent of those people lived in rural areas where many if not most of them were able to be largely independent by living off the land.

Our nation's founders were concerned about maintaining our freedom as a nation. They were concerned also with ensuring that the various states worked together to develop laws, policies and institutions that would provide equal treatment under the law for all citizens. Additionally, because many of the original colonists had come to this new land seeking freedom from state-imposed religions, it was important to them that government not impose any one particular religious belief or practice on its citizens.

But our founding fathers simply did not and could not have imagined the diversity of our population today and the problems of racial, ethnic or sexual discrimination that have come with such diversity. They could not have imagined today's multinational corporations. Or our international banking system. Or the problems of air and water pollution. Or of climate change. Or the implications of radio or of television, let alone the Internet revolution!

They also could not have imagined a country of 50 states whose territory extends nearly 3,000 miles from ocean to ocean, south to Puerto Rico and the U.S. Virgin Islands in the Caribbean Sea, north to Alaska and westward across the Pacific Ocean to Hawaii, and still another 3,800 miles west to the island of Guam and 2,300 miles south from there to American Samoa. Nor could they have imagined a country with a population of more than 300 million people, only 20 percent of whom now live in rural areas.

Similarly, they could not have imagined the absolute necessity of educating all of our populace. Or the range of skills and knowledge required for most jobs in this modern world. At the time of Thomas Jefferson, Benjamin Franklin and George Washington, only the wealthy were well-educated. The common people were lucky to learn how to read, write their names and do simple sums. And, in fact, most people were not that lucky.

Similarly, they could not have imagined a society that of necessity must consider the social well-being of all of its citizens if it is to ensure "domestic tranquility." In the 18th century, few people outside of the local areas would ever hear of families starving in rural Pennsylvania or South Carolina. Or of someone being murdered in Virginia. Or of severe flooding in some distant area. And not because no one would care, but because they did not have the communications systems that exist in this, the 21st century.

Our society today is so much more complex, so much more integrated and blessed (or, perhaps, cursed) with instant communication 24 hours a day and seven days a week that it is simply impossible for our federal government to play the limited role that many people would like. We could not survive as a country.

The fundamental fact that anyone with even a modicum of common sense knows in his or her gut is that we cannot go back to simpler days – not even to the simpler days of the 1950s. We must instead deal with the reality of today – a reality that is both complex and changing. Moreover, our government must adapt to that reality. And that government must also, of necessity, be complex and evolving.

Let's think for a moment about the many roles our federal government must fill.

Interestingly, although the framers of our Constitution could not possibly have imagined our world as it is today, they could and did think about the roles of the government they were framing – roles brilliantly described in the Preamble to our Constitution:

"We the people of the United States, in order to form a more perfect Union, establish Justice, insure domestic Tranquility, provide for the common defense, promote the general Welfare, and secure the Blessings of Liberty to ourselves and our Posterity, do ordain and establish this Constitution of the United States of America."

Let's look at those roles in the context of today.

First, let's consider national defense or, as I prefer to call it, national security. To our nation's founders, this meant protecting our land from other nations that might want to take it over. It also meant protecting our commerce on the sea. But the only weapons available in those days were cannons, muskets, rifles, spears and bows and arrows.

Today, our government must think of national security in a variety of ways. War, for example, can include conventional battlefields and conventional weapons. It can also include nuclear, biological and chemical weapons. Moreover, as we have seen particularly in the past 15 to 20 years, it can include terrorism and fanatics willing to blow themselves up if they can kill and maim others in their suicide attacks.

But national security in today's world is not limited to violent warfare or terrorism. Our economic well-being is a vital component of national security. For that reason, our federal government must be able to protect us from trade wars declared and undeclared. It must not allow our need for energy – particularly for oil and gas – to be used as a weapon against us. And in this world of computers and the Internet, it must protect us also from cyber warfare.

Our national security also involves protection from natural and manmade disasters. While government cannot prevent hurricanes or floods, it can mitigate the effects of those natural phenomena by affecting our preparedness and our response. Similarly, while government cannot be expected to prevent outbreaks of flu or other diseases, it can be expected to work effectively to minimize the effects of such potential disasters.

In the area of manmade disasters, government can protect us from the poisoning of our waterways, our groundwater and the air we breathe as the result of industrial activities. It can help us mitigate the effects of our activities on the global climate and protect our food supply from contamination. It can also protect us from economic collapse caused by excesses in the capitalist system of economics that we have embraced.

All of these examples describe legitimate functions of government in the 21st century in its role of providing "for the common defense" — a role clearly stated in the Preamble to our Constitution.

Next, to "insure domestic Tranquility," we need a strong and active federal government to protect minorities against the excesses of the majority. This includes not only minorities as we think of them traditionally – e.g., by race, sex or sexual orientation, culture or ethnic origin – but also religious and political minorities.

To "establish Justice" as well as to ensure domestic tranquility and to "promote the general Welfare," we need a strong federal government to protect not only the "rights" of individual citizens against the intrusion of government, but also to protect individual citizens against the powerful private institutions that have flourished in our modern economic and social system. The most recent economic downturn demonstrated all too vividly what happens when predatory (or "greedy") corporations or business people are allowed too much freedom to operate. The runaway costs of our health care system have demonstrated what happens when that system – most of whose components are interested primarily in making money – is allowed too much freedom to operate. And, to a large extent, the failures of our public education system demonstrate what happens when there is little or no public accountability – accountability that must be coordinated at a national level if it is to be effective.

And, finally, we need a strong federal government to ensure there is a minimum uniformity of laws and practices among the various states. Yes, the states are self-governing to a large degree. But they are also integral parts of the whole. And one critical role of the federal government is to ensure that the states work together toward the national good and that citizens moving from one state to another do not, for the most part, suddenly find themselves facing a different set of laws as they cross state lines.

Now, having tried to make the point that it is absurd to argue for a return to a smaller federal government, let me address what seems to be a primary concern for many people: That government is becoming too intrusive, involving itself too much in business, education, health and many other areas.

First, I understand that concern. I too want to be able to live my life without Big Brother telling me what to do. But at the same time, I understand that we are a society of more than 300 million people – people with a wide range of capabilities. And the plain fact is that all of our citizens need protection from predators. Think for a minute about the home mortgage debacle we have gone through in recent years.

Hundreds of thousands of Americans were offered mortgages when the mortgage brokers making those offers knew full well that many of the people accepting those mortgages would be unable to sustain them. These so-called subprime mortgages were "justified" on the grounds that they offered families who normally would not qualify for mortgages the opportunity to own their own homes. Talk about holding candy in front of a baby!

The mortgage brokers also aggressively marketed adjustable rate mortgages with very low teaser interest rates to people who already owned their homes. These homeowners were encouraged to take the equity out of their homes (thereby increasing the amount of their mortgages) so they could use that money for other purposes. All the while, the mortgage brokers knew full well that when the interest rates of these mortgages were adjusted upwards, the likelihood was that many people would be unable to afford the higher payments.

The banks also knew that many of these mortgages were questionable. In many instances, people weren't even asked to submit financial statements before being approved for their mortgages. Wall Street also knew that many of these mortgages could not be sustained over the long haul. And the mortgages – both good and bad – were bundled together in packages and sold to Fannie Mae and other institutional investors – i.e., to other financial institutions. In many cases, the investors took out insurance on these bundled mortgages, making me suspect that even these institutional investors knew that many of these mortgages were likely to go into default.

In other words, greed was running amok and the major players in the financial industry were gambling big time. The mortgage brokers – the sales people who were initiating these mortgages in the first place – were among the lucky ones. They got paid their commissions right away and many made fortunes. Financial industry executives made out just as well; they got their multimillion-dollar bonuses even after their bad decisions led to a major financial crisis. The rest of us paid the price when the economy collapsed, the bottom fell out of the housing market, millions of people lost their jobs and/or homes, and the United States fell into the worst recession in 80 years.

Now, let me say for the record that I know I have oversimplified what happened. I also know that many people argue that individuals must to take responsibility for their own decisions. For example, the people who took the equity out of their houses and accepted adjustable rate mortgages should have known that they would be unable to meet the mortgage payments when their interest rates were adjusted upwards.

But here's where "should" and "shouldn't" bump into reality. First, most people are not financially sophisticated. Secondly, not all people are equally bright. If the average IQ is 100, that means that half of the population has an IQ of 100 or higher and half of the population has an IQ of 100 or lower. Not only that, but many people with high IQs are not financially savvy. What this means is that many people almost certainly did not understand and *could not have been expected to understand without a lot of good advice* the full implications of the mortgage agreements they were signing.

Equally important, we Americans are fundamentally optimists. We may not know today how we will make those higher interest payments two or four years from now, but we believe in ourselves and we face the future with confidence. I know this because I am one of those people. Throughout my adult life, I have based a number of financial decisions on the assumption that I would receive regular pay increases as I advanced in my career, or that my investments would increase in value. This part of the American character may not excuse bad decision-making by people who in fact should have known better, but it makes it more understandable.

Nevertheless, the point I am making remains valid. "We the people" were the victims of a predatory banking system *whose leaders and minions were interested only in enriching themselves and were willing to work the system to their own advantage.* They didn't care about the impact of their actions on their customers. And, they didn't even consider the potential impact of their actions on the "general welfare" of the nation as described in the Preamble to the Constitution.

In other words, without a strong and active federal government to stand between the public and the banking system, we are at its mercy. The same is true of the health insurance industry – both "for-profit" and "non-profit" insurers – whose primary motivation has always been and remains today the making of money, not public health. Moreover, this same truth applies to most or all of the many other large institutional organizations that form the economic fabric of our society.

Of course, it should be understood that the desire to "make money" is not bad or evil. That motivation is what makes our economic system work. What it means, however, is that someone – in our case, the federal government — must place limits on the activities of these institutions to ensure they function in the broad public interest as well as in their own narrower self-interests.

We also need a strong federal government to protect our individual rights. We are a multi-cultural society. Our people come from a broad diversity of racial and ethnic backgrounds. And we are a nation whose citizens have many different religious beliefs. Our federal government has made great progress in taking steps to ensure equal protection under the law for all of its citizens, and to bring an end to institutional racism and sex discrimination. But we need to do more.

For the past 30 or more years, a strong movement has been afoot to impose the religious views of certain groups of people on the nation as a whole. The most obvious target of this campaign has involved abortion rights.

One cannot deny that the campaign to make abortion illegal or to make access to abortion more difficult in the United State has its basis in the religious views of its proponents. But the question I keep asking myself is this: What right do people have to impose their religious beliefs about this or any other issue on me or the rest of the country by demanding that the Law of the Land (or of individual states) reflect their religious viewpoint? Why is it that everyone must respect their religious beliefs about abortion, for example, but they are not required to respect the beliefs of others who would allow abortion? And what right under the Constitution does Congress or any other legislative body or any court have to impose the practical effect of any groups' religious viewpoint on this issue on the nation as whole?

To those who argue that many of the laws in Western society have a basis in religion going back to the Ten Commandments, I would suggest another possibility. While it is certainly possible that Moses received the Ten Commandments from God as described in the Bible, it is equally possible that he was simply a very smart man who realized that he needed to establish an authority greater than his own to impose a set of practical rules necessary for his people to survive their trek through the desert. And so he claimed that they came from God.

In either case, the Ten Commandments represent a fundamental and pragmatic set of rules that any tribal society would need to survive. Thou shall not kill. Thou shall not steal. Thou shall not covet thy neighbor's wife. Thou shall not commit adultery. Even the commandment about having "no other God before me" is a pragmatic rule needed to avoid internal strife in any tribal society although experience suggests it is the antithesis of a pragmatism for avoiding strife in a multicultural society or world.

Again, think about it: It has been said that more people have been killed in religious strife over the centuries than from all other conflicts throughout history. And, as we know all too well from our daily news reports, killing in the name of religion is still going on today – not only in far-off lands, but in our own country (See Chapter 16 – Religion Gone Awry).

So let's come back to the role of government. And to the size and intrusiveness of government.

My common sense tells me that this government – as Abraham Lincoln so aptly described it – this government "of the people, by the people and *for* the people" should be pragmatic.

Guided by the value system established in the Declaration of Independence and in the Constitution of the United States of America, Congress should enact laws only because they have a pragmatic value in enabling us to flourish individually and collectively in a peaceful and orderly manner. That statement applies to all parts of our society – laws affecting individuals directly as well as laws affecting individuals indirectly by regulating the institutions within our society. It also applies to laws affecting our country's functions within the larger community of nations.

Just as the value system established in our Constitution requires us to respect the cultural, ethnic and religious diversity within our own society, that same value system should require us to respect the cultural, ethnic, political and religious diversity within the community of nations. That means, for example, that we should not undertake as a national mission to convert the world to "democracy" or to any particular religion. We should instead treat the rest of the world as we (hopefully) treat our own diverse population – with respect and dignity — and in a manner that will encourage all nations to thrive while recognizing our need to protect our own national interests and safety.

I submit that this is not a prescription for small government. Or for passive government. Or even for a completely unintrusive government. It is, however, a prescription for an effective government in today's world and the future. And it is a prescription for a government able to fulfill the ultimate role described in the Preamble to our Constitution: to "secure the Blessings of Liberty to ourselves and our Posterity."

Taxes: Too Much or Too Little? – Part I

5

Preamble to the Constitution of the United States of America

We the people of the United States, in Order to form a more perfect Union, establish Justice, insure domestic Tranquility, provide for the common defense, promote the General Welfare, and secure the Blessing of Liberty to ourselves and our Posterity, do ordain and establish this Constitution of the United States of America.

I have reproduced the preamble to our Constitution above because I am concerned that the three-legged stool described earlier has, in fact, becomes so unbalanced that it will fall over in the not-so-distant future unless major effort is undertaken to bring it back to a stable position – effort that must go far beyond the measures described in earlier chapters.

In other words, I believe we are facing a potential for major social unrest and upheaval in our nation. And I'm not talking about movements like the Tea Party, though when those folk realize what's actually happening in our country, those same people may well be a part of the upheaval.

I do not believe I am being alarmist. Look at the numbers and trend line and decide for yourself what will happen if this trend continues.

In the past 28 years, the distribution of wealth in this country has shifted dramatically in favor of the wealthy. According to a study reported in USA Today, the share of income in the United States "going to the richest 1 percent (of Americans) rose from less than 10 percent in 1980 to nearly 20 percent in 2008-12."[3] This increase, the paper reported, "was among the most dramatic increases in wealth disparity (in the world).[4]

In terms of net worth, as recently as 2010 – the last year for which I have found numbers – the wealthiest 1 percent of our population represented more than 35 percent of the nation's total net worth (including the net value of people's homes). The wealthiest 20 percent of our population – and that includes corporate management, professionals (doctors, lawyers, etc.) and small business owners along with the wealthiest 1 percent – accounted for nearly 89 percent of the nation's total net worth.

This means that the net worth of the rest of us – the other 80 percent of people, the wage and salary earners – represented barely more than 11 percent of the nation's total (Table 1).

Looking one layer deeper, the working people, whose net worth represented nearly 19 percent of the total in 1983, have seen their share of the national net worth pie cut by more than 40 percent in the 28-year period from 1983 to 2010. Moreover, the slow recovery from the recent recession with its lost jobs, the spate of mortgage foreclosures and the dramatic drop in home values has hurt wage

[3] USA Today, January 21, 2014 – Page 1 "In global wealth, 85 = 3,500,000,000"
[4] Ibid

and salary workers far more than it has hurt the wealthier segments of our population. As a result, the working person's share of the nation's net worth has almost certainly grown even smaller by now.

Table 1[5]

Distribution of Net Worth in the United States 1983-2010

Year	Top 1%	Top 20%	Bottom 80%
1983	33.8%	81.3%	18.7%
1989	37.4%	83.5%	16.5%
1992	37.2%	83.8%	16.2%
1995	38.5%	83.9%	16.1%
1998	38.1%	83.4%	16.6%
2001	33.4%	84.4%	15.6%
2004	34.3%	84.6%	15.3%
2007	34.6%	85.0%	15.0%
2010	35.4%	88.9%	11.1%

Note: Net worth is defined as total assets minus total liabilities. Total assets are defined as the sum of (1) the gross value of owner-occupied housing; (2) other real estate owned by the household; (3) cash and demand deposits; (4) time and savings deposits, certificates of deposit, and money market accounts; (5) government bonds, corporate bonds,

---

[5] Table I is adapted from a similar table in *Who Rules America?* by Professor G. William Dumhoff, Sociology Dept., University of California at Santa Cruz. http://www2.ucsc.edu/whorulesamerica/power/wealth.html

foreign bonds and other financial securities; (6) cash surrender value of life insurance policies; (7) cash surrender value of pension plans, including IRAs and Keogh and 401(k) plans; (8) corporate stock and mutual funds; (9) net equity in unincorporated businesses; and (10) equity in trust funds. Total liabilities are the sum of (1) mortgage debt; (2) consumer debt including auto loans; and (3) other debt.

The picture is even bleaker from the viewpoint of working people when financial wealth is considered – that is, what's left after taking their homes out of the picture. In 2010, the wealthiest 1 percent of our population owned more than 42 percent of the nation's financial wealth. The wealthiest 20 percent – and, again, that includes corporate management, professionals (doctors, lawyers, etc.) and small business owners along with the wealthiest 1 percent – owned a whopping 95.3 percent of the nation's financial wealth.

What that means is that the rest of us – the other 80 percent of people (in other words, the working people) – were left owning only 4.7 percent of the nation's financial wealth (Table 2). Again, that disparity has almost certainly grown worse as a result of our slow recovery from the recession.

Table 2[6]

Distribution of Financial Wealth in the United States 1983-2010

Year	Top 1%	Next 19%	Bottom 80%
1983	42.9%	48.4%	8.7%
1989	46.9%	46.5%	6.6%
1992	45.6%	46.7%	7.7%
1995	47.2%	45.9%	7.0%
1998	47.3%	43.6%	9.1%
2001	39.7%	51.5%	8.7%
2004	42.2%	50.3%	7.5%
2007	42.7%	50.3%	7.0%
2010	42.1%	53.5%	4.7%

NOTE: Financial wealth is defined as net worth minus the value of one's home.

* * *

In the report referenced here, Professor G. William Dumhoff of the University of California at Santa Cruz, added telling detail to these columns of numbers. "In terms of financial wealth, the top 1 percent of households have 35 percent of all privately held stock, 64.4 percent of financial securities, and 62.4 percent of business equity. The top 10 percent have 81 to 94 percent of stock, bonds, trust funds, and business equity and almost 80 percent of non-home

---

[6] Table 2 is adapted from a similar table in *Who Rules America?* by Professor G. William Dumhoff, Sociology Department, University of California at Santa Cruz. http://www2.ucsc.edu/whorulesamerica/power/wealth/html.

real estate. Since financial wealth is what counts as far as the control of income-producing assets (is concerned), *we can say that just 10 percent of the people own the United States of America* (emphasis added)."

Another section of the report looks at the distribution of wealth by race and ethnicity, comparing the total wealth (including home equity) and the financial wealth (excluding home equity) of white Americans, African-Americans and Latino-Americans. The numbers are discouraging. Quoting Professor Dumhoff: "In 2010, the average white household had almost 20 times as much total wealth as the average African-American household, and more than 70 times as much wealth as the average Latino household. If we exclude home equity from the calculations and consider only financial wealth, the ratios *are more than 100:1* (emphasis added)."

Consider this last fact in light of this information from the Census Bureau: Today, African-Americans represent nearly 14 percent and Hispanic Americans about 16 percent of our country's population. By the year 2050, non-Hispanic white Americans will represent less than 47 percent of the population, according to Census Bureau estimates.

I am concerned that the combination of this continuing trend of wealth concentration into the hands of an elite and small segment of society, of reports that many of the same people in the financial industry who helped cause our economic meltdown by their bad decisions have been rewarded for those bad decisions with multi-million dollar bonuses...of reports that CEOs continue to receive astounding pay packages (such as the CEO of Ford Motor Co. receiving a pay package totaling $54.6 million for one year or the CEO of United Health Group, Inc. receiving total compensation of

$106 million for one year at a time when we had 14 million people unemployed)...of the continuing efforts by many members of Congress to cut federal programs that help people on the low end of the socio-economic ladder...of state governments forcing teachers and other state employees to take pay cuts in efforts to balance their budgets...and, more recently, the shutdown of the federal government because many members of Congress refused to approve a budget without further cuts in domestic programs...I am concerned that all of these sooner or later will lead to widespread frustration and anger among the tens of millions of people who feel they are getting the short end of the economic stick.

Too often, I think, many if not most Americans focus only on their "rights" as enumerated in the Bill of Rights as the important part of the Constitution. Those rights are important. The key words for this discussion, however, are in the Preamble to the Constitution quoted at the beginning of this chapter. The reasons our founding fathers gave for creating our Constitution are found in those words: "to form a more perfect Union," "to insure domestic Tranquility," and to "promote the general welfare..."

Who six months earlier would have predicted the upheaval in Egypt, Bahrain, Libya and Syria in the first months of 2011? And don't try to tell me that such upheaval and violence can't happen in the United States of America! Few if any of us can remember personally the violent labor riots in the late 19th and early 20th centuries. But many of us can indeed remember the riots in our cities in the late 1960s. I certainly do. I was a young reporter at the time and helped cover those riots in my hometown.

The point I am making is this: This kind of violent social turmoil erupts when people have been pushed too far. And I believe we are approaching that flash point in our country because our corporations and the wealthy people who control them have become too powerful and too greedy. We have, in fact, allowed capitalism so much free rein that we are putting our nation at risk.

In the area of tax law, corporations have so successfully influenced congressional legislation to change tax laws in their favor that General Electric Corp. made the headlines in 2011 because the company paid no federal income tax on their 2010 corporate earnings of $14.2 billion, $5.1 billion of which was earned directly from its U.S. operations – this at a time when our government was dealing with a huge revenue shortfall and many in Congress were – and still are – attempting to cut domestic programs that benefit the poorest among us.

And General Electric is not the only corporation to pay little or no income tax on billions of dollars in profit.

It is time to change corporate tax laws.

To begin with, it is absurd that corporations are able to maintain two sets of books – one for tax purposes and one for reporting to stockholders. One immediate change in corporate tax law should require corporations to pay taxes on the profits they report to stockholders. In other words, if General Electric reports $14.2 billion in profits to stockholders, it would pay $3.87 billion in federal income taxes at current corporate tax rates.

Secondly, we should do away with the notion that corporations can shield all or part of their income from U.S. taxes by moving their legal place of domicile to another country or by shifting operations overseas. The profits of any company or any offshore affiliate or subsidiary of a U.S. corporation that sells its products or services in this country should be subject to U.S. corporate income taxes.

Thirdly, regulations surrounding the issuance of work permits (green cards) to foreign workers must be tightened greatly. Today, theoretically, such work permits are issued only when a company certifies that there are no qualified personnel available in the U.S. work force for positions it wants to fill. Those regulations should be changed to require a significantly higher standard of proof that there are no U.S. citizens who are either qualified immediately or *who could be trained in a reasonable period* to fill employment vacancies in the company's U.S. operations. Importing workers from outside the United States should be a last resort, not a first.

And finally, I suggest that any time a U.S. company shifts production overseas to take advantage of lower overseas labor costs, thereby putting U.S. employees out of work, the products produced overseas by that company for sale in the United States should have import duties imposed upon them to offset the lower production costs obtained by the company. We simply cannot, as a nation, afford to allow corporations to export our jobs in their never-ending quest for higher profits. Corporations will argue that such tariffs will make consumer products cost more. But the price we pay for lower prices on imported goods – the loss of U.S. jobs – is too high.

Our country has almost been taken over by corporate interests and wealthy citizens whose greed leads them to support the unbridled corporate quest for profits. It is not only time for corporations to pay higher taxes for the service our government provides in creating and maintaining an environment that allows them to prosper, but for wealthier citizens to begin paying their fair share of those taxes as well.

One final note: It is argued by some that efforts to increase taxes on wealthy citizens are an attempt to redistribute wealth. The fact is this: The practical effect of *any* change in income tax law is to redistribute wealth. And, as the data clearly show, the tax cuts favoring wealthy taxpayers over the years since the Reagan-era tax cuts of the 1980s have themselves resulted in a dramatic redistribution of wealth by increasingly concentrating it in the hands of the wealthy.

If we are to preserve our "more perfect union" by ensuring "domestic tranquility" and promoting "the general welfare" as envisioned in the Preamble to our Constitution, then we must reverse the present trend of wealth concentration and work our way back to a more equitable distribution of wealth. Moreover, all taxpayers, including our corporations, must provide the revenue required to fund all government operations.

Taxes: Too Much or Too Little – Part II

6

The fact that taxes are one of the most controversial political issues in this country should come as no surprise. Our nation has a long history with this issue.

It was the "tea tax" imposed by Britain on the American colonies that gave rise to the Boston Tea Party before the Revolutionary War. And it was a tax on whiskey passed by the first Congress of the United States that led to the so-called "Whiskey Rebellion" in the early 1790s and provided the first test of the primacy of the federal government in disputes with the states.

Still, even knowing this history, I am always amazed by how intensely some people resent paying taxes. One neighbor once commented that he felt as if the government was putting its hand in his pocket and stealing his money.

Let me lay my biases right out on the table. First, I believe that *everyone* should pay some amount of taxes to government. Yes, I said *everyone.* That's why, for example, I support sales taxes at the state level and would support a modest national sales tax.

Let me explain: If we use only a personal income tax, excise taxes like those on tobacco and alcohol (which are invisible) or taxes on business to fund our government, then all of those individuals whose incomes are too low for them to pay personal income tax are deprived of the opportunity to participate knowingly in the financing of their government.

But a sales tax gives everyone – even the poorest person – the opportunity to contribute to the financial support of government *even if that person gets money from the government in some form of tax credit, welfare, food stamps, etc.* That person still gets to participate in the financing of his government every time he or she makes a taxable purchase.[7]

I can hear the comments now: "This guy is crazy!"

No, I just believe that each of us has a variety of obligations as a member of society and as a citizen or future citizen of our country. One of those obligations is to contribute to the support of our government.

Secondly, I think we should scrap the words "income tax." Instead, we should call our payments to government an "income-based fee for service" – the fee we pay government for the service of ensuring a stable society in which we can live in peace and harmony and where each person has the opportunity to achieve to the limits of his capabilities.

It is, after all, government that provides the structure this motley collection of people, states, territories, etc., requires to survive as a country. It is government that provides the structure that enables us as individuals to pursue our dreams. It is government that provides the structure that allows us to create and build wealth. Moreover, this government is one that we have developed for ourselves and that "We the People" direct through our participatory democracy.

---

[7] I would prefer a national sales tax over the oft-mentioned "value added tax" because it is less complicated, probably less costly to administer and more visible – that is, the person has the tax added to his purchase at the cash register. In addition, that sales tax should exclude food, medications, shelter and services.

If you doubt any of these statements, consider this question: If it is not the environment, structure and system provided by our government through our Constitution that has enabled the amazing growth of our country and its economy, then why haven't other countries experienced the same kind of growth and prosperity? Why is America called the "Land of Opportunity?" And why is it that we have drawn people from all over the world to our shores – people who are seeking a better life?

No, the question is not *whether* we should pay taxes. The question is *how* those taxes should be structured. And, when considering our tax structure, two primary considerations emerge.

First, it is vitally important to our country that tax laws encourage the growth of a large and prosperous middle class. And that they do so in a way that allows even the poorest person to believe he can build a better future for himself and his family by dint of hard work.

This is crucial. It is crucial because one of the most important factors in maintaining a stable and prosperous United States of America is the existence of a strong middle class. Not only do we need a prosperous and large middle class to provide the purchasing power essential to fuel our economy, but we also need that strong middle class to provide the fundamental stability that anchors our entire social system.

I remember vividly during the years of the Cold War, for example, hearing the frequent claim that the primary reason we did not have to worry about communism taking hold in the United States was that we had a strong middle class. In fact, the only time that communism gained even a toehold in this country was during the Great Depression of the 1930s.

Communism thrived on class warfare, in which the wealthy

aristocrats were perceived as feeding upon the "under classes." But the very existence of a large, growing and prosperous middle class in the United States after World War II put a lie to the claims of class warfare, at least in our country.

For the record, I am not trying to raise the bogeyman of communism. What I am trying to do is to illustrate the importance to our social and economic well-being of tax policies that support the growth of a strong middle class.

Unfortunately, it seems obvious to me that the Reagan tax revolution, particularly as revisited by Republicans during the second Bush presidency, has proved detrimental to the goal of encouraging growth of a strong middle class. In fact, since the year 2000, changes in the structure of our federal income taxes have helped increase the disparity between the wealthy and the rest of society, with a resulting shrinkage in the strength of the middle class.

Second, it is critically important that the tax structure be perceived by the public as "fair."

Such is not the case today. The common public perception is that a combination of loopholes and schemes available to wealthy individuals to shelter their incomes enables the rich to avoid paying taxes while ordinary low and middle income taxpayers are at the mercy of the system.

I share that perception.

Common sense also suggests that our federal income tax system has been structured to favor the wealthy. Perhaps it didn't start out that way, but that is how it has evolved.

Let me offer the example of the "capital gains tax."

In theory, the very low tax rate on capital gains from so-called long-term investments in the stock market is intended to encourage investment in new or expanding businesses so that those businesses can grow and prosper, create more jobs and generally contribute to the economic growth of the country. The low tax rate is justified because the investors are "risking" their money to help the economy grow.

Reality is far different. Only a tiny – miniscule – amount of the money invested in the stock market is actually used by any company to help it grow or to create new jobs. Moreover, most new companies are underwritten today by so-called venture capitalists long before their stock is listed on any stock market and it is the venture capitalists who are risking their money.

No, the fact is that most of the stocks traded every business day on the various stock exchanges have been in circulation for years – many of them for decades. And the stark truth is that the stock market is really little more than a casino on a grand scale. But gamblers who "play" the stock market get special tax treatment – unlike gamblers in a more conventional casino, who are supposed to pay the same tax rates on their winnings that they pay on their earned income.

This, I submit, is an example of a tax law that was put into place for a valid purpose but has now become obsolete as the world has changed. As a result, the primary beneficiaries of our capital gains tax laws as they are now structured are not new or expanding businesses, but mostly gamblers "playing" the stock market.

While it is true that millions of middle- and even lower-income Americans are stock market investors through mutual fund investments in their 401ks, IRAs and pension plans, it is the wealthy investors who make the largest amounts of money in the stock market simply because they have the most money to invest.

Moreover, people with money in 401k, traditional IRA or pension accounts do not get to take advantage of the capital gains tax rates. They pay ordinary income tax rates when they withdraw money from those accounts. As a result, on an individual basis, it is primarily wealthy investors (read "wealthy stock market gamblers") who benefit from the very low, long-term capital gains tax rate – an assertion backed up by Professor Dumhoff's report showing that the wealthiest 10 percent of Americans own more than 80 percent of stocks and mutual funds.[8]

What should be done? Common sense would suggest that Congress change the capital gains tax laws to focus them on their original purpose by limiting special tax treatment to 1) new stock issued by start-up companies to raise capital to repay their start-up indebtedness or to raise capital for expansion, or 2) new stock issued by established companies specifically for the purpose of funding expansion of their businesses (but not including stock issued to provide bonuses to employees).

Another example: Our marginal tax rates also now favor the wealthy. This was not always the case. In the 1960s and '70s, tax rates for the wealthy were truly onerous. I can remember my father, who was not wealthy but instead was part of the growing middle class, saying that he did not want to receive any more promotions in his job because the marginal tax rates were so high even at his income level that the added stress and responsibility would not be worth the net after-tax increase in his monthly check.

For information, in 1963 the top federal income tax bracket was 91 percent for single taxpayers with taxable income of more than $200,000. That means that 91 of every 100 dollars in taxable income

---

[8] "Who Rules America?" by Professor G. William Dunhoff

above $200,000 went to the federal government. Married taxpayers faced the same high rate on taxable incomes of more than $400,000. Moreover, in some states, taxpayers had to pay state income taxes on top of that. Just about everyone would agree that such tax rates were excessive!

By the time Ronald Reagan became president in 1981, the top tax bracket had come down to 70 percent, but was still too high. By the time Reagan left office, the top bracket was down to 28 percent, which was too low. It was a typical pendulum swing, from one extreme to the other.

I don't really want to get into a debate about how high rates should or should not be, but it seems clear to me that the marginal tax rates on the wealthy should be significantly higher than they are today and that wealthy taxpayers should not be able to shelter ordinary income – earned income – from taxes.

None of that income should be able to be sheltered by other schemes, including: the awarding of stock options to corporate executives with the expectation that the executives receiving those options will be able to pay taxes at the lower capital gains rates when any income from those options is finally received; or losses from other investments. In other words, paper losses from such things as real estate tax shelters should not be deductible from earned income. Although losses from investments could be used to offset gains from other investments, they should not be deductible from earned income.

Additionally, as suggested above, the practice of offering special "capital gains" tax rates to people who play the stock market should be scrapped. Gamblers in the stock markets should face the same taxation on their "winnings" as people who play the slot machines, craps, blackjack or roulette in casinos. Their gains should be taxed as ordinary income; their losses should not be deductible.

Finally, to those who object to paying their fair share of taxes or who oppose increasing the tax burden on our wealthier citizens, I say this: "It's called 'payback.' And now, it's payback time."

Paying taxes is the price you pay for living in a country that allows you and, in fact, enables you to become wealthy. If you have been fortunate enough to become wealthy, it is time for you to give something back to the country that made it possible. And one way you do that is by paying your fair share of taxes. My common sense tells me that is "the American way." Americans don't just take. They also give.

Having said that, I am very much aware that the wealthier segments of taxpayers already provide a large fraction of the total income tax revenues received by the federal government. But that shouldn't be surprising, not when the wealthiest 20 percent of our population owns more than 95 percent of the country's financial wealth! But rather than arguing against higher taxes on the wealthy, they should be advocating those higher taxes because it is in wealthier citizens' self-interest to pay substantially more than they do now. But I'm not asking them to write blank checks.

When President Clinton left office, our national budget was balanced and, in fact, was running a surplus. Tax revenues were greater than expenditures. Six major events occurred in succeeding years that have combined to cause most of the very large budget deficits our government is running today. Those include: the September 11 terrorist attack, which had a profound effect on our national psyche and economy; the war in Afghanistan; a reduction in income tax rates enacted in 2003; the war in Iraq; the hurricane devastation along the Gulf Coast; and the economic meltdown in 2008.

Those six events combined to form the "perfect budgetary storm." Although most of those events may have been unavoidable, the huge deficits could have been prevented if we'd had the political courage to prepare for them ahead of time. And we can still do something about them today.

Here's what is needed.

First, the tax rates on earned income and the tax brackets enacted in 1993 should be restored. Although current rates for wealthier taxpayers are similar, the brackets make them more favorable to wealthy taxpayers than those of 1993. The key point is that our country was doing just fine with the marginal tax rates that were in effect during the last years of that decade.

Second, the capital gains tax on stocks should be limited to stock newly issued by start-up companies or by existing companies to raise capital to fund expansion as described earlier. This would enable stock market gamblers to treat their winnings as regular income and corporate executive to include income received from stock options in their pay packages as regular income. In addition the capital gains tax rates should be restored to the 1993 levels.

Third, we need legislation that will provide for contingency tax increases (possibly in the form of a surtax on personal and corporate income taxes) to be put into effect by the president to pay for the costs of unbudgeted military activity and/or of unexpected social costs resulting from natural disaster or economic recession so that we don't face this same problem again.

The contingency tax need not be sufficient to offset 100 percent of the unexpected cost immediately, but it should be sufficient to pay down that cost within a very few years after the military activity, natural disaster and/or recession has ended. To ensure that Congress is not giving the executive branch an unrestricted license to tax, the legislation should include a one-year sunset provision after the contingency tax increase has been put into effect unless Congress affirms the president's decision by a majority vote. With congressional affirmation, the increase would remain in effect until the unexpected expenditure has ended and been paid for.

Fourth, let me revisit my earlier argument for adoption of a national sales tax. Without a national sales tax, a significant percentage of our citizens have no opportunity to contribute consciously and directly to the financial support of their national government. Not only do I believe they deserve that opportunity, but one common complaint heard about the income tax is that so many people get off scot-free because they don't have to pay income taxes. There is no logic to that complaint, but it plays into the importance of the appearance of "fairness" in the system. A system of taxation that includes a modest national sales tax so that everyone is paying taxes to the government is on the face of it fairer than the present system. Moreover, that sense of "fairness" would be increased if the national sales tax were made deductible (as are state sales taxes) on personal income tax returns.

Fifth, we should require that each year's budget contains a provision to retire some modest amount of national debt.

And finally, we need a balanced budget law. This law should accomplish three things: (1) It should require the president to present Congress with tax proposals to pay for budgeted requests if those requests exceed the then current year's expected revenues; (2) it should require that any budget passed by Congress include provision for tax revenues sufficient to cover budgeted expenditures; and (3) it should require that any extra-budgetary expenditures subsequently approved by Congress contain provisions for generating the revenue required to pay for them.

Where would this money come from? Obviously the bulk of the money would come from wealthier citizens and corporations. However, by legislating provisions for the contingency tax in the form of a surtax on personal and corporate income taxes, that burden would be spread among all taxpayers. If higher revenues are required to support normal budgetary items, it will be up to the president or Congress to recommend a source for those revenues.

Additionally, I believe each of our 50 states should also enact provisions for a contingency tax to help them get through tough economic times.

It is as certain as the fact that the sun rises in the east and sets in the west that the states are going to experience economic ups and downs. Few state legislatures have ever made sufficient provision for weathering serious economic storms. Some states have "rainy day funds," but such funds have limits. When they are depleted, the state is left with only the options of cutting back on services or raising taxes. Politically, raising taxes is nearly impossible in the middle of a recession. As a result, it is services that get cut and state employees who often get no raises, take cuts in their pay or get laid off. And in every state, the services that get cut are services to the least powerful among us.

There is, however, a better alternative: Enact a contingency sales tax that would be held in abeyance during normal times but would go into effect in an economic downturn to cover budget shortfalls caused by otherwise declining tax revenues. In states that already use a sales tax to raise revenues, the contingency tax would be in the form of an additional 2 or 3 percent added to the existing tax rate. In other words, in states with a 6 percent sales tax, the added contingency tax would raise the rate to 8 or 9 percent. In states without an existing sales tax, it would be a new – but temporary – 2 or 3 percent sales tax.

Why a sales tax? First and foremost, a sales tax in the least painful tax for the public to pay because it is paid a few pennies or dollars at a time. If a 2 or 3 percent contingency sales tax were added to all of their purchases (excluding food and medicine), most people would barely notice it. Second, a sales tax is a broad tax. That is, everyone pays it. And finally, even in recessionary time, although people don't spend as much, they do keep spending. So the contingency sales tax is guaranteed to generate revenue.

I am confident that most voters would much rather pay another two or three cents per dollar in sales tax during tough economic times than have cutbacks in care for the elderly in their homes, cuts in teaching staff at public schools, cuts in police, fire and prison budgets, or cuts in funding for other essential services. And even if some voters would be unhappy, if a state is suffering a budget shortfall in a recession, state employees should not have to shoulder that burden by themselves. Basic fairness dictates that the burden should be spread among all of the state's citizens.

Moreover, if the contingency tax were enacted during good years and held on standby during good times so that it is seen as a safety net for leaner times, the political downside would be small. And, when those leaner times occurred and the extra sales tax kicked in to enable state governments to avoid major cutbacks in programs, most voters would be applauding the foresight of their legislators.

There is, however, one other requirement for such a tax. There must be specific triggers to put the contingency tax into effect, and for ending it so that it can be put back in storage for the next time it is needed.

My suggestion is that this tax be triggered both on and off by the unemployment rate. For example, if a state's unemployment rate were to climb above 7 percent and stay there for a minimum of six months, the contingency tax would go into effect. Similarly, as the economy improved and the unemployment rate dropped below 7 percent and stayed there for a minimum of six months, the tax would be canceled or phased out.

There is one other area of our system of taxes I would like to address – the use of special purpose taxes to help curb certain business excesses.

The use of tax policy as an instrument for achieving desired national goals has a long history. One example is the capital gains tax, when used properly. Other examples from our personal income tax laws include the deduction for home mortgage interest to encourage home ownership and the deduction for charitable contributions to encourage taxpayer financial support of charities.

Recently, we have seen tax credits used both to encourage the purchase of more energy efficient appliances by homeowners and to encourage businesses to invest in their own renewable energy systems to provide all or part of the electrical needs for their offices, warehouses and manufacturing facilities. We've also seen special tax credits to encourage first-time home buyers to help boost the housing market out of recession.

Those examples, of course, involve the use of individual and corporate income tax incentives to achieve national goals. A variety of special purpose taxes are also used to achieve national goals.

Over the past decade or two, for example, we've seen increased taxes on tobacco products implemented for two purposes – to make smoking more expensive and, hopefully, less desirable; and, to help pay for the very large medical expenses incurred by Medicare and Medicaid patients from smoking-related health problems.

Other longtime examples include the gasoline tax used to help fund highway construction and, at the state, county and local levels, property taxes to fund public school operations and to pay for construction of new schools and other public buildings.

All of these are what I call "special purpose taxes." And, they serve valid functions.

What I am proposing is a new set of two narrowly focused special purpose taxes specifically designed to curb or offset one of the very costly negative side-effects of capitalism in the pursuit of profit – that is, the incredible growth of obesity in these United States.

These special purpose taxes would have three goals: (1) to provide incentive for targeted businesses to redirect their pursuit of profit toward a more socially beneficial goal – i.e., a healthier citizenry; (2) to provide a financial incentive for individuals to adopt healthier eating habits; and (3) to offset some of the huge health care costs incurred by Medicare and Medicaid because of our obesity epidemic. The two taxes are a "fat tax" and a "sugar tax."

Before I address each of these taxes individually, let me explain how it is that they address capitalism taken to an extreme.

First, it is a given that all aspects of our food system are part of our capitalist business system. At all levels of the system, individuals and businesses are striving to maximize profits. Food companies are competing with one another to attract customers to their products, and most of them do this by attempting to make their products as appealing as possible.

How do you make food appealing? The easiest ways are to increase serving size, add more salt, fat and/or sugar, or do all of these. In southern-style cooking, vegetables are cooked with pork and pork fat to make them taste better. Deep-fried food has become de rigeur nationwide – even such things as deep-fried Oreos and deep fried candy bars. Even traditional Thanksgiving turkeys are being deep-fried.

Sugar is added to all kinds of foods whether or not it is needed. Breakfast cereals have been pumped up with sugar and are promoted with sugary names – Kellogg's "Honey Smacks", for example, which are 55 percent sugar by weight.

The point I am trying to make is that most food companies – including processed food manufacturers, fast food chains and many restaurants – have gone to such extremes in their use of salt, fat and sugar in competing with one another for customer dollars that our society has become unhealthily overweight. Many fast food chains and restaurants have similarly gone to competitive extremes by offering larger and larger servings. And we are paying for it through our health care system.[9]

Those are the excesses of capitalism these two proposed food taxes are intended to address.

First, what I call the "Fat Tax."

Let me acknowledge that in some ways this is an "off-the-wall" idea. I do wish, however, that I could claim the idea as my own because

---

[9] I must acknowledge that some food and beverage companies are attempting to remove calories from the marketplace. In a voluntary effort, 16 companies in 2010 pledged to cut 1 trillion calories from their offerings by 2012 and 1.5 trillion calories by 2015. According to the Associated Press in a report January 9, 2014, the companies had surpassed their pledged goal by a wide margin, cutting daily calorie intake by an amount equal to 78 calories per person nationwide. I applaud the effort, but believe stronger steps are required.

it makes uncommonly good sense. It is not, however, my idea. Instead, I first heard this idea from one of my daughters who wrote a tongue-in-cheek newspaper column several years ago about a proposal in her state legislature for a large tax on tobacco products. She wasn't serious in her suggestion. I am, however, completely serious in mine.

Before rejecting the idea out of hand, think about it for a moment.

An estimated 70 percent of Americans are significantly overweight. The health care costs to the nation from this high rate of obesity are enormous. Moreover, under our current system, taxpayers end up paying for nearly 50 percent of all health care costs,[10] including those related to obesity. The new health insurance laws may ameliorate some of this taxpayer burden, but much of it will remain.

So the question is this: Why shouldn't the people who overeat simply because it makes them feel good and who eat food that is blatantly unhealthy ... why shouldn't those people help pay directly for the health care costs obese people incur instead of dumping nearly half of their medical care costs on taxpayers in general?

Think about it: Many fast food outlets now compete to see who can offer the biggest hamburgers. They "super-size" servings of french fries for a small additional price. And they do these things to compete with other fast food outlets. And to attract people who will buy those things.

To discourage that kind of unhealthy eating, I'd like to see a 25 percent federal fat tax on hamburgers that exceed the usual standard serving size for ground beef of 4 ounces. That tax would be in addition to normal sales taxes. The revenues from the fat tax also would be

---

[10] From "Uninsured will keep health care costs up" by Gregory Warner, reported on "Marketplace," National Public Radio, January 28, 2010

specifically directed to subsidize Medicare, Medicaid and any other public health insurance programs.

Hopefully the fat tax would make those burgers so expensive that people would stop eating them. Realistically, it wouldn't stop everyone, and some people would just buy two smaller burgers, but at least those who wanted to eat those burgers badly enough to pay for them would be subsidizing the health care of obese people. And the fact of the fat tax might make some consumers more aware that such large servings are unhealthy.

But I wouldn't stop there. I'd put a fat tax on all deep fried food, including potato chips and corn chips. I'd also tax vegetables cooked with pork so that vegetables are flavored with the pork fat. I'd also tax the fat content of ground meat by establishing a level of fat that was acceptable and imposing the fat tax on ground meat with a higher fat content. Grilled or baked lean meats, poultry and fish would be exempted from the tax.

As for prepared foods, I would put a fat tax on all prepared foods in which fat accounts for more than 25 percent of the calories per serving. I would also require restaurants and retail stores selling these high-fat foods to list the fat tax clearly on receipts so that purchasers could see how much that unhealthy fat content is adding to their bills. It should even be possible to have receipts show specifically which foods incurred the tax.

Such a tax – especially if receipts included information as to which foods incurred the fat tax – would also help educate people about what foods are unhealthy. In restaurants, foods that incur the fat tax could be labeled as such on the menus (much as low-carb or low-calorie items are now labeled on some menus) so that diners could make informed decisions when ordering their meals.

Okay, that's one way to use a new tax to advance a national goal of reducing both the rate of obesity and the taxpayer burden of paying for obesity-related medical costs. Here's another – one that has already been floated unsuccessfully in Congress: a tax on the sugar content of foods.

Before you reject this idea out of hand, consider the following: Prepared-food companies (including bakers and juice and soft drink manufacturers as well as makers of canned food, sauces and various entrees, side dishes, and desserts) have deliberately used sugar in their foods to increase their appeal – whether or not sugar in that quantity is necessary or, in fact, whether sugar is even an essential ingredient in that food.

The problem with this, of course, is that these companies have essentially trained our taste buds to want sugar – more sugar than comes with many fresh foods naturally, and certainly more sugar than was in foods consumed by previous generations.

For example, when I was a youngster, we had Wheaties, Corn Flakes and a few other breakfast cereals. If we wanted to sweeten our bowl of cereal, we sprinkled sugar on it. And our parents let us know if they thought we were using too much sugar! Since that time, sugar has become a major ingredient of most breakfast cereals. Although the Kellogg's Honey Smacks example I mentioned earlier is an extreme, cereals containing sugar representing from 30 to 40 percent of each bite by weight are common.[11]

---

[11] Every package of cereal has a display listing the serving size in ounces and grams and the quantity of various ingredients, including sugar, also by weight in grams. If the serving size is 30 grams and each serving contains 12 grams of sugar, the sugar content of that cereal is 40 percent by weight. In the Kellogg's Honey Smack cereal mentioned about, the serving size is 27 grams and the sugar content per serving is 15 grams, or a bit more than 55 percent by weight.

Many of these foods could be made with less sugar or even very little sugar and they would be equally appealing as our palates adjusted. In fact, the manufacturers could probably reduce the sugar content in small increments over a period of months and few people would notice the difference.

The goal of the sugar tax, of course, would be the same as the goal of the fat tax – to help reduce obesity and related health problems and to defray obesity-related health care costs.

Initially, when I considered this idea, I thought it would be more difficult to design and administer a sugar tax than a fat tax. But when I learned that sugar represents as much as 50 percent by weight on some breakfast cereals, I had a "Eureka" moment. Simply tax each product – and here we're talking about prepared and/or packaged foods – by the percentage of sugar by weight above a certain untaxed maximum established for each category of product.

So, for example, if the untaxed maximum level of sugar established for breakfast cereal were 10 percent by weight, then a breakfast cereal that is 50 percent sugar would have a 40 percent sugar tax placed on it (40 percent of the price of the cereal) and be itemized on store receipts as suggested for the fat tax. If the cereal had a sugar content of 15 percent by weight, the sugar tax would be 5 percent of the price.

In time, by making sugar-loaded foods more expensive, hopefully, people would switch to lower sugar content products. Moreover, I suspect that food companies would quickly begin reducing the sugar content of their products to reduce the tax burden on those items as a means for making their cereals more price competitive. And, hopefully, we would become healthier as a nation for it.

One final comment about taxes: Over the past 30-plus years –

since the beginning of the Reagan presidency and the rise of conservative opposition to taxes – many members of Congress as well as state and local elected officials and legislators have been reluctant to raise taxes and, in fact, have often pledged in their campaigns for office not to do so. In many cases, the result has been failure at the federal, state and local levels to align tax revenues with needs for services.

I think it is time for all politicians to take a new look at taxes. Taxes themselves are not evil or bad. They are necessary for government to fulfill its many roles in our complex society. If our politicians could step aside from their political ideologies, take a fresh look at the role of taxes, and become creative in structuring our taxes so that they not only provide needed revenue but also are perceived as fair, we could solve a lot of problems.

This two-part discussion of taxes has offered a few of my suggestions. They may or may not be the best ideas around. But we have serious budgetary problems in this country at all levels of government. So far, all I've heard anyone do is point fingers and lay blame. I'm tired of that. More importantly, pointing fingers doesn't solve problems. We need people who will sit down and search for pragmatic solutions. I'm trying to get that process started.

America's New Indentured Servants

7

Credit card banks in the United States have created a new class of indentured servants. But there is a major difference between the indentured servants of the 21st century and those of the 17th and 18th centuries.

When the American colonies were being established, many people with no money to pay for their passage from Europe to the colonies (and many who were more or less shanghaied) entered into agreements that required them to work for their patrons in the colonies for a set number of years – usually from four to seven years – in exchange for their passage and upkeep during those years.[12] At the end of that agreed-upon time, they were freed of all obligation and able to build their own futures in the New World. Those were the indentured servants of that era.

Today's indentured servants are Americans who have built up often staggering amounts of credit card debt. Why do I call these credit card holders modern "indentured servants"? Consider this: It will take a card holder with a $3,200 credit card debt who can make only the minimum payment each month at least 15 years – more likely 25 years or longer – to pay off that debt.

By doubling that payment, the same cardholder could pay off the

---

[12] I should note also that many if not most of those indentured servants in the American colonies in the 18th century endured harsh conditions of servitude during their periods of indenture.

debt in three or four years. The problem, however, is that many people have multiple credit cards, each carrying a balance, and the cardholders can only afford to make minimum payments. Moreover, depending upon their available cash after paying for living expenses every month, they may be making those minimum payments for all of those 15 or more years.

There are two reasons it can take so long to pay off credit card debt. One is that minimum payments are deliberately set low by the credit card companies. By doing so, the credit card companies not only make the debt more attractive to consumers because of the low monthly payment, they also stretch out the payments so that they (the banks) can collect more interest. The second reason it takes so long to pay off the debt is that credit card debt carries very high interest rates (Table 3).

Typically, there is one interest rate for debt incurred from credit card purchases, a second higher interest rate for credit card cash advances, and a third still higher rate – now called the "penalty rate" – paid by cardholders who are late with a payment. Although it is possible to work one's way out of the penalty rate by making at least the minimum payment on time for six consecutive months, being irregular in making payments can result in a person paying the penalty rate until, after as many as 24 years, the loan is paid off.

All of these rates are often two, three or even four times the rate your local bank, for example, is legally allowed to charge for a car loan. The high credit card interest rates are justified with the argument that they pose higher risk to the credit card companies because they are "unsecured." With a car loan, the lender can repossess the car if the borrower misses payments. The credit card company can only keep sending out monthly bills.

But common sense suggests that we ask this question: "Who creates the risk?"

Is it consumers who say, "Thank you very much" when credit card companies offer them preapproved credit cards and they begin to use those cards? Or is it the credit card companies who create the risk by extending those lines of credit without requiring financial statements from the prospective cardholder?

Table 3. Typical Credit Card Interest Rates As of January 2014

	Purchase Rate	*Cash Advance Rate*	*Penalty Rate*
Discover			
	Prime + 9.74%	Prime + 20.74%	Prime + 26.74%*
Bank of America			
	Prime + 10.99%	Prime + 20.99%	**
Chase			
	Prime + 12.99%	Prime + 15.99%	29.99%
Capital One			
	Prime + 14.65%	Prime + 21.65%	Prime + 26.15%
American Express			
	14.50% (Variable)	25.24% V***	27.24% V***
Citicard			
	19.99% (Variable)	21.99% V***	29.99% V***

Note: Interest rates may vary among different cards issued by the same bank.

* Discover Card has different penalty rates for purchases and cash advances. The rate shown is the higher rate for cash advances.

** At this writing, a Bank of America customer service person explained after consulting with her management that the bank does not have a predetermined penalty rate for its credit cards. Instead, the penalty rate is determined individually for each cardholder who falls into default, taking the cardholder's history and other risk factors into consideration.

*** All of these rates are designated as "variable," which means they will go up or down as the prime rate goes up or down.

* * *

Taking this question one step further: Who creates the risk when a credit card company mails blank checks to cardholders that can be used for taking cash advances with ultra-low teaser interest rates – even 0% interest for 12 months? Is it the cardholder? Or, is it the credit card company?

Just a little common sense would suggest that credit card companies create their own risk in the same way that mortgage brokers who sold the subprime mortgages that led to the collapse of our financial system in 2008 created the mortgage industry's own risk. They sold adjustable rate mortgages with very low teaser rates to people who would not under any normal circumstances qualify for those mortgages.

Worse yet, those mortgages were often approved without requiring a financial statement from the borrowers – borrowers who the mortgage brokers knew full well would probably be unable to make their payments when the interest rates were adjusted upwards again and again. The only way for a homeowner to escape that interest-rate escalator was for the homeowner to obtain a fixed-rate mortgage – something the subprime homeowner would be unable to do.

There has been, however, a huge difference between the "risk" taken by credit card companies and the "risk" taken by the mortgage industry. The risks taken by the mortgage industry were quite real, as we discovered painfully. The "risk" taken by credit card companies, on the other hand, has been illusory – a phantom risk created to justify their high interest rates.

In fact, credit card companies have been taking no risk at all. The extremely high interest rates they've been allowed to charge cardholders have guaranteed their profits even if some cardholders defaulted completely. And, when cardholders deeply in debt began turning to personal bankruptcy to get out from under their crushing debt, the banks successfully lobbied Congress to have bankruptcy laws changed to close that escape hatch with passage in 2005 of the Bankruptcy Abuse Prevention and Consumer Protection Act. Among its provisions, this legislation makes it much more difficult than before for people to file for personal bankruptcy, particularly because of consumer debt.

Let's look at facts.

First, a minimum payment on a credit card bill is typically 2 percent or less of the outstanding balance. Second, a typical interest rate for purchases is currently about 15 percent per year, or about 1.25 percent per month.

In this typical situation, therefore, the minimum payment for someone who has a balance of $3,000 on his credit card would be

$60 (2 percent of $3,000). The first $37.50 of that payment would go to pay interest (1.25 percent of $3,000), leaving only $22.50 to go toward reducing the debt. If the minimum payment is less than 2 percent, the amount going toward the debt will be even less.

The banks have one other trick built into the system. As the balance gets lower, the minimum payment is reduced. In the example above, after two payments, the minimum payment would be lowered to $59.00, reducing the amount paid toward principal by another dollar. And so it would go.

The practical effect is that it will take anyone with $3,000 in debt on that credit card from 15 to 20 years to pay it off by making only the minimum payments – *if and only if he puts that credit card away and doesn't use it again until the loan is paid off. And if and only if the cardholder always pays the bill on time so that no late fees or penalty interest are added to the account. And more important, if and only if the interest rate stays the same.*

The last point is perhaps the most important point.

Congress in its "wisdom" enacted legislation in 2008 that placed several restrictions on the activities of credit card companies – restrictions that took effect in 2010. The purpose of the law, among other things was to protect consumers against arbitrary interest rate increases and the industry's "previously" harsh default rate practices. The law has provided some protection against the former default-rate practices, but it has done almost nothing to protect cardholders against interest rate increases.

Let me explain.

To get around the law's intended restrictions on rate increases, most of the major credit card banks have created a two-part interest rate. One part is the so-called "index rate" controlled by the credit card companies – which, if this system is ever challenged in court, will argue that the index rate is the portion of the interest rate that is regulated by law. The second part, over which the companies have no control, is the "prime rate," which fluctuates with the federal funds target rate adopted by the Federal Reserve Board. This two-part system means that the interest rates that credit card companies charge their cardholders are thus the sum of the index rate and the prime rate. If the prime rate rises, the interest charged to credit card holders also rises.

From a practical viewpoint, what this means is that consumer credit card interest rates will go up and down as the Federal Reserve Board raises or lowers the federal funds target rate. And again, if this system is ever challenged in court, the credit card companies will argue that the 2008 law applies only to the index rate portion of their interest charges because that is the only portion over which they have control.

It is noteworthy that when the companies adopted this new method of calculating cardholder interest rates, the prime rate was not only at an historic low, but was as low as it will ever get – 3.25 percent.[13] Thus, when the credit card companies adopted their new method of establishing credit card interest rates, they were effectively establishing a floor for what they will charge their cardholders.

Where is that floor? Pretty high when you consider that a typical credit card index rate ranges from 10.99 to 14.99 percent for purchases and from 15.99 to 21.99 percent for cash advances. With the prime rate at 3.25 percent, those add up to interest rates ranging from 14.24

---

[13] The prime rate is typically about 3 percentage points above the federal funds target rate. Thus, a prime rate of 3.25 percent means that the federal funds target rate was between 0 and 0.25 percent – i.e., essentially zero.

to 18.24 percent on debt created by making purchases and from 19.24 to 25.24 on debt from cash advances.

Now here's the kicker: Historically, the Federal Reserve has attempted to maintain its federal funds target rate at around 3 to 4 percent. That translates to a prime rate of 6 or 7 percent, which in turn, using the examples above, translates to credit cards interest rates ranging from 17.24 to 21.24 percent for purchases and from 22.24 to 30.24 percent for cash advances during more "normal" economic conditions.

But the 3 or 4 percent federal funds rate is a target. In reality, the rate fluctuates enormously as the Federal Reserve moves that target up and down in its efforts to control inflation. For example, in the early 1980s, the prime rate was as high as 21.5 percent. With the system the credit card companies are using now to calculate interest, that would have translated to credit card interest rates as high as 36.49 percent for purchases and 43.49 percent for cash advances.

In the mid-1980s, the prime rate ranged between 7.5 and 13 percent. During the 1990s, the prime rate was fairly consistently in the 6 to 9 percent range. In the 00s, it was generally in the 4 to 8 percent range.

The point is this: The combination of high index rates set by the banks and variations in the prime rate as the federal funds target moves up and down can really hurt credit card holders. Yes, the rates will move down as well as up. But in this case, down means only that those rates will be "less high". Up means they will be exorbitant!

One other point must be made here as well. Almost no one has only one credit card. Many people carry balances on multiple cards and make minimum payments on all of those cards. So their debt is not simply $2,000 or $3,000 on a single card. It might be $2,000 or

$3,000 or $6,000 or $7,000 or even more on each of several cards. And, under the present system, they will be making minimum payments against that credit card debt for many years and, possibly for the rest of their lives.

That's why today's credit card debtors are America's new class of indentured servants.

It can be argued, of course, that cardholders are free to pay more than the minimum each month and, therefore, pay off the debt faster. But let's be realistic: First, most people who create significant credit card debt are having trouble making ends meet (they are spending every penny or more than they earn) and are unlikely to pay more than the minimum payment required. Second, the fact is that millions of people have been given very large credit lines by credit card companies and, as a result, have built up such high levels of debt that they can only afford to make minimum payments.

Third, few people with credit card debt put their cards in a drawer and stop using them. Either they keep on using the existing cards, in which case they will never pay off those accounts, or they accept new cards and create still more debt.

Some observers will argue that people drowning in credit card debt have no one to blame but themselves. "They should have known better than to spend so much more money than they could afford."

While that argument has some validity, it's what I call a "morality" argument and has no place in this discussion. Morality arguments deal with "shoulds" and "should nots." They do not solve problems. They merely allow the people making those arguments to feel superior. I want to deal with the problem that exists and to find pragmatic, common sense solutions to that problem.

Moreover, I disagree with that morality argument on an even more fundamental basis.

First, as noted earlier, not everyone is equally smart when it comes to handling money.

Second, our business community – corporate America – through its marketing and advertising activities over recent decades has created a society accustomed to instant gratification. Moreover, the marketing of credit cards has played a major role in creating that instant gratification environment. “You don’t need money in your pocket to purchase whatever you want; you can just charge it now and pay for it later!”

Third, credit card companies have aggressively marketed their cards. Even in the middle of the recent recession – from 2008 onward – our household has continued to receive unsolicited offers of “preapproved” new credit cards. The banks have sent out literally hundreds of millions of unsolicited credit card offers (often with preapproved credit limits) every year for the past 20 or 30 years, making it unbelievably easy for people to amass lines of credit that in aggregate are far higher than any responsible bank loan officer would approve if those same people were to apply for an unsecured line of credit from their bank. In fact, I recently learned of a married couple who were asking their parents for help because they had accumulated credit card debt of $160,000!

Beyond that, these same credit card companies have aggressively marketed credit card cash advances at zero percent, 1.99 percent, or other extremely low interest rates good for six or eight months – or even as long as 14 months – knowing full well that many people taking advantage of those offers will be unable to pay off those cash advances before their interest rate changes to the prevailing rate – now typically ranging from 16 to 22 percent, but certain to go higher as the economy recovers and the prime rate is increased.

In fact, that's precisely how the banks can afford to make those offers. They know that while they might make no money or even lose money during the period of the low teaser rate, they will more than make up for that loss once the high cash-advance rate is applied to the unpaid balance.

When I say that these cash advance offers have been marketed aggressively, I mean AGGRESSIVELY in capital letters. For example, not a month has gone by – even in the midst of recession – that our household has not received along with our credit card bills blank checks that we could use to initiate a credit card cash advance for any amount up to our available credit limit. Most often those checks are accompanied by offers of extremely low cash advance teaser rates (as long as you pay your bill on time) for periods ranging from two to 12 months. In addition, we have received regular separate mailings every month containing offers of low teaser rates and blank checks that can be used for balance transfers or, presumably, for a simple cash advance.

In a time of recession and slow recovery such as we have experienced in the past several years, with people losing their jobs and needing money to pay bills, or in a time of stagnant wages and a steadily rising cost of living as through the first seven or eight years of this new century, it is very understandable that people would reach for the lifeline of easy credit card cash advances to help them make ends meet until they can get a raise, a higher-paying job, a second job, or even just simply get a job to replace the one they lost when the greed of large banks, mortgage brokers, Wall Street derivatives traders, etc. brought about the collapse of our financial system and the resulting recession.

No, this is not a moral problem. It is a human problem affecting millions of people and it needs solving.

Okay, so what do we do about it?

First, we need to look at how we got into this mess. Knowing that, we can figure out what to do about it.

The situation has its roots in the small state of Delaware's desire in 1980 to diversify its economic base and the desire of major banks to be freed from interest rate restrictions on their credit card operations. The result after meetings between bank and state officials was the state legislature's passage of the Financial Center Development Act early in 1981. Specifically, the purpose of this legislation was to lure credit card banking operations to Delaware.

And it worked – Big Time!

With the passage of this Delaware law, banks began moving their credit card operations to Delaware, bringing thousands of jobs to the state, large new multi-story office buildings into the city of Wilmington, and, of course, increased revenue to both the city and state. According to the Delaware Economic Development Office, the financial services sector of Delaware's economy has grown to include "more than 1,000 employers and more than 40,000 employees." Moreover, in 2005, according to an article in *Fortune* magazine, Delaware housed six of the ten banks with the highest volume of credit card lending.

How did little Delaware do this?

Well, in many ways. But the biggest attraction to the banks were several specific provisions of the Financial Center Development Act: First, it permitted out-of-state bank holding companies to establish specialized subsidiaries in the state to house their credit card operations; second, it eliminated interest rate limits on credit card debt (at that time, most states limited credit card interest rates to 12 percent) and allowed banks both to charge fees for their credit cards and to change the terms of their credit card agreements at will; and third, as if all of that were not enough, the state sugar-coated the legislation by establishing a regressive tax rate so that the more money the credit card operations made, the lower their tax rate – all the way down to 2.7 percent.

The result for Delaware was an economic boon. The result for the nation as a whole, however, was to unleash the credit card industry because, with the stroke of Governor Pete du Pont's pen on that legislation, the credit card business was turned into a cash cow for the banks.

As a result, the credit card industry ballooned. In 1980, the total credit card industry was represented by some 129 million cards and about $24 billion in loans. Twenty years later, there were nearly a BILLION credit cards in people's hands and total loans of $538 billion. Moreover, in the year 2000, consumers received more than 3.5 BILLION credit card offers in the mail![14]

Did I mention that banks have marketed their cards aggressively?

Okay, that's how we got into this situation. The question now is this: How can we get out of it? How can we free the millions of modern indentured servants here in America and, at the same time, create an environment that will allow the credit card industry to make reasonable profits?

The first step is to impose, at the federal level, a cap on interest rates. No one should face paying 30 percent or even 18 percent interest on debt when, as of this writing, the prime rate is 3.25 percent. My suggestion is to establish a cap on the index rates that banks can

---

[14] The News-Journal, Wilmington, Delaware. January 28, 2001 – Pages 1 and 8

charge. Earlier, I said that a typical index rate ranged from 10.99 to 14.99 percent for purchases and from 15.99 to 21.99 percent for cash advances.

I believe those rates are excessive. In fact, I would call them usurious. Instead, I'd suggest federally mandated maximum but fluctuating credit card interest rates of prime plus an index rate of 5 or 6 percent for unsecured debt (purchases and cash advances) and a penalty rate of prime plus 8 or 9 percent, with both rates being reset monthly as is the current practice. This would allow credit card companies to count on a constant but reasonable profit margin and protect consumers from excessive rates.

The second step is to require fixed minimum payments based on the highest level of debt. In other words, the minimum payment would not be reduced as the debt declined. Those payments should also be high enough so that the debt can be paid off in a reasonable period of time – say, a maximum of five or six years. (This second requirement, however, should apply only to new debt created after the change goes into effect.) If a cardholder wants to continue using the card while making payments so that he pays interest indefinitely, that's his choice. But if he wants to eliminate that debt, the payments should be structured to make that possible.

The third step is to bar banks from sending out unsolicited offers for preapproved credit cards. They certainly should be able to invite consumers to *apply* for one of their credit cards. But I would require credit card companies to use the same approval process their local bank branches would use to extend any other unsecured loan, such as an unsecured line of credit on a checking account.

This means requiring the credit card companies to review a complete financial statement and to take into consideration the number of credit cards a person already owns and the aggregate credit lines of those cards. Along with this, banks should be forbidden to increase credit limits without a review of the card holder's up-to-date financial statement.

Finally, Congress should repeal provisions of the 2005 Bankruptcy Abuse Prevention and Consumer Protection Act that have made it so difficult for people to file for personal bankruptcy, particularly for consumer debt. The banking industry lobbied hard for years to have those changes made to prevent their overburdened credit card holders from using personal bankruptcy to get out from under their debt. But for many people, bankruptcy was then and, realistically, is today the only way out from under their accumulated debt – debt the credit card industry deliberately and consciously set out to create using all of the marketing tools available to it.

A cap on interest rates, higher minimum payments, a ban on unsolicited credit card offers, and higher standards for approving credit limits will help prevent abuses going forward. They will not, however, be sufficient to help many of our current 21st century indentured servants work their way out of servitude. For those people, personal bankruptcy may be their only road to freedom.

Credit card companies will consider these proposals draconian, but one role of government is to protect the public from powerful predators. Moreover, there is no question that the credit card companies have evolved into powerful predators by using the lure of easy credit, low monthly payments and aggressive marketing programs to indenture millions of Americans, thereby turning America into a debtor society.

It is, however, time for change. The societal price we have paid and will continue to pay in coming years if the credit card companies are not reined in is too high. We need to re-establish reasonable limits on credit card interest rates and to establish realistic and prudent standards for companies to follow in issuing credit cards. If we do this, the credit card companies will adapt to the new rules and they will continue to prosper, though perhaps not quite as wildly as they do now. As important, many consumers will have the opportunity to work their way out of their indentured servitude and into a new-found financial freedom. And for those for whom these reforms are not enough, restoring personal bankruptcy as a realistic option is an obvious goal and Congress should do it.

Finally, to those who argue that credit cards have fueled the economic boom since the early 1980s, I agree. It was, however, an economic boom built on sand, not on solid footings. All of the credit card debt that fueled those boom years must be repaid – with interest. And money that goes toward paying that debt and interest is money that is unavailable for purchasing consumer goods or service. Yes, it stays within the economy, but it does not add to the economy in the same way that it would if those dollars were being spent to purchase the goods and services that fuel real economic growth.

But we can fix that. We can create a new economic boom built on solid rock by changing the laws governing credit cards along the lines I am suggesting. All it requires is a common sense approach to the problem and the moral courage to act upon it

The War on Drugs

8

The problem of illegal drugs is one in which the moral issues of drug abuse have gotten in the way of any possible solution.

What do I mean? Simply this. If you view drug abuse as a moral problem or as a criminal problem (in this case, morality and criminality being two sides of the same coin), you limit the solutions to morality and the criminal justice system. And that, in effect, is what we have done.

We have been waging a "War on Drugs" for more than 30 years. We have spent well over $100 billion in just the past ten years alone attempting to deal with the societal problems of drug abuse and to stop the trafficking in illegal drugs (Table 4).

What have we accomplished? We have criminalized the possession and use of drugs. We have taken away judicial discretion in the sentencing of drug offenders, providing for mandatory minimum sentences for anyone found guilty of a drug offense. And we have filled our local, state and federal prisons often above their intended capacity. And the problem has only gotten worse.

Table 4.

National Drug Control Budget (aka "War on Drugs Budget")

2008	$13.7 Billion
2007	$12.8 Billion
2006	$12.4 Billion (requested)
2005	$12.2 Billion
2004	$12.033 Billion
2003	$19.2 Billion (requested)
2002	$18.8 Billion
2001	$19.2 Billion (requested)
2000	$18.5 Billion
1999	$17.1 Billion
1998	$16 Billion

Source: The National Criminal Justice Reference Service

* * *

It's truth time.

Nothing we have done in the past 30 years has slowed the trade in illegal drugs one iota. Oh, we've moved it around. While we have made progress in combatting drug cartels in Colombia, new drug lords and gangs have appeared in Mexico and elsewhere. In essence, we have been playing Whack-A-Mole, the game in which you hit a mole on the head and pound him into the table only to have another mole pop his head out another hole. But all the while, the drug lords have grown richer as the tentacles of the drug-abuse octopus have reached farther and farther into our society, even into the smallest and most-remote towns and cities.

Frankly, our focus on the morality and criminality of the illegal drug trade has blinded us to the most important and profoundly simple fact about the illegal drug trade: It's a business!

The illegal drug trade is a textbook example of capitalism at work. Drug entrepreneurs pay small farmers in poor agrarian societies to grow their raw materials, which the entrepreneurs convert into a product in widely scattered production facilities and then distribute through a chain of wholesalers to retailers on the street. And, as in any integrated business activity, there is profit at every level. Moreover, the profits from the sale of illegal drugs in the United States alone are many billions of dollars each year.[15]

As in every business activity, of course, there are costs of doing business. Payoffs to politicians, judges, police and border guards are normal business expenses. Losing product in drug busts or police drug seizures is another cost of doing business. And, having employees go to jail is still another cost of doing business.

There is even a form of marketing. We call it "pushing." We call the retail salesmen "drug pushers." And – here is the point – these street retailers are *pushin*g their drugs into every large and small community in our country using all kinds of marketing tricks to get our children hooked at ever-younger ages.

This is a classic business structure. It is a classic business strategy. It is a classic marketing strategy. And, it works just as effectively for the illegal drug trade as it does for any other business organization.

Moreover, there is only one way to fight it: On business terms. We have to compete with the drug cartels in the marketplace and

---

[15] More than 20 years ago, the retail value of illicit drugs in the United States was an estimated $40 billion to $50 billion, according to a June 1991 technical report of the Office of National Drug Control Policy.

drive them out of business by making high-quality drugs legally available at little or no cost, undercutting the drug cartels' prices and taking away their profits.

But this comes with a prerequisite: As a society, we must get off our moral high horse and recognize that drug abuse – like cigarette smoking and alcohol abuse – is a public health problem, not a moral or criminal problem. In the same way that we have accepted that a certain percentage of our population will become addicted to cigarettes or to alcohol, we must accept that some unknown percentage of our population will become addicted to other drugs. And, accepting that fact, we must deal with drug abuse in a constructive manner.

If we can do that – or, perhaps, as we are coming around to accepting that – we must also take the next step: Legalizing the sale of the major drugs – marijuana, heroin and cocaine – and making them available *legally* at a cost that undercuts the price of all illegal drugs. In effect, we must go into competition with the drug cartels and take the profit from their business. That is the only way we can put these drug cartels out of business in the United States of America.[16]

Finally, we need to redirect much of the money now allocated every year for the so-called "war on drugs" to neighborhood drug clinics where addicts can get drugs free or priced on a sliding scale based upon the individual's income. We also need to build a network of neighborhood treatment centers throughout the country where existing and future addicts have treatment readily available to help them overcome their addiction at a price they can afford – or at no cost if necessary.

---

[16] In effect, we are getting our toes wet with this approach by the legalization of marijuana in a few jurisdictions.

Most importantly, we must do all of this in a way that is non-judgmental and is completely non-threatening. It will do no good to offer free or low-cost drugs if people who come for them are publicly stigmatized. And we must ensure that addicts who are still able to work will never feel their jobs are threatened if they take advantage of public clinics. Otherwise, they won't "come out of the closet" to take advantage of the legal drugs or treatment centers, but will instead continue to support the illegal trade.

Helping existing addicts by making drugs available to them legally and offering treatment for their addiction are perhaps the most important steps we can take to undercut the illegal drug trade. People who are already drug-addicted provide the primary customer base for that illegal trade and we need to take that customer base away from the drug lords, pure and simple. Finally we need to decriminalize drug possession and use. We also need to move people whose only offense has been possession or use of illegal drugs out of prisons and into rehabilitation centers, offering them the proverbial "clean slate" to help them reenter society in a constructive manner, not as ex-cons. We should definitely maintain criminalization of both the manufacture and sale of illegal drugs. But we've got to stop putting people in jail simply because they have become addicted to drugs.

Now, I can already hear the cries of protest. And I know where they will come from.

First the protests will come from people who believe that use of drugs is immoral and that we as a society cannot abase ourselves by legalizing them.

Second, the protests of the law-enforcement community may well be just as loud as that of the moralists.

Let's take a look at these two major sources of opposition to legalizing drugs one at a time.

First, the morality lobby. I have written elsewhere in this book that I believe moral arguments do not solve societal problems and may, in fact, aggravate them. We should have learned that lesson with Prohibition nearly a century ago. The moral arguments against legalizing drugs are essentially the same arguments that brought about Prohibition in 1919 and the subsequent rise of bootleggers, organized crime and the gang violence of the 1920s and '30s.

Prohibition also turned otherwise law-abiding citizens into "criminals" by making the mere possession of alcohol for personal use in your home a federal offense. Even my own father, an otherwise completely law-abiding and highly moral person, told tales of making bathtub gin in the 1920s and early '30s. Had he been caught, he would have been arrested.

Fortunately, the Prohibition nightmare lasted only 14 years. In 1933, the production, sale and possession of alcoholic beverages were legalized and Prohibition repealed, ending that nightmare in our history (though some states and local communities retained their own "prohibition" laws well into the second half of the 20th century).

Clearly morality arguments and criminalization failed to work with alcohol during the Prohibition era and we can see all too clearly that they have failed to work in the 30-plus years of our own "War on Drugs" – a phrase first used by President Richard Nixon in 1971, but really brought into the public consciousness and vernacular by President Ronald Reagan in the 1980s.

For example, as a result of our morality approach to this problem – that is, by criminalizing possession and use of marijuana and other illegal drugs – we have filled our prisons beyond their intended capacity and some states have been forced to release felons to the streets early because their prisons are overcrowded.

Think about that. And while you're thinking about it, add in the fact that one of every two inmates in our federal prisons, one in five inmates in state prisons, and one in four inmates in local jails are there because we have criminalized drug abuse.[17]

And think about this: It costs U.S. taxpayers more than $22,000 per year per inmate to house each drug abuser in state and federal prisons. And, when that person gets out of prison, he is often unemployable (who hires ex-cons?), will likely end up back on the street and may well end up back in prison.

Meanwhile, we have seen no reduction in our drug problem. Quite the contrary. The problem has only grown worse. In short, the moralist approach simply hasn't worked.

Now to the protests of the law enforcement community: Who do you think has been one of the largest beneficiaries of the billions of dollars the federal government has poured into the War on Drugs over the last 30 years? Right!! The law enforcement community.

In fiscal year 2007, for example, more than half of the $12.8 billion federal budget for the war on drugs went to underwriting various components of the criminal justice system.[18]

Frankly, law enforcement agencies at the federal, state and local levels all have a vested interest in maintaining the status quo in our approach to the problem. If funding for the war on drugs were reduced dramatically by diverting the funds to drug clinics and local treatment centers, many of these law enforcement organizations would face major budget crises.

Never mind that our jails are overflowing because of the

---

[17] Source: Bureau of Justice Statistics
[18] Ibid.

incarceration of drug offenders. And never mind that this 30-year "war on drugs" has been completely ineffective in its goal of reducing the flow of illegal drugs into our country. And never mind that after 30 years of the war on drugs, the illegal drug industry still has one of the largest single sales forces in America working hard every day to achieve an ever-greater market penetration.

It's just common sense. Pouring more money into law-enforcement efforts to fight an ill-conceived war on drugs will do no good. That doesn't mean we should cut off federal aid to state and local law-enforcement agencies. But a measured approach to reducing federal funding of anti-drug police work over a period of years while building up an infrastructure to support the legal sale of abused drugs and the development of expanded low-cost or free local treatment programs to deal with drug abuse is certainly warranted.

And frankly, local crime rates will almost certainly drop if these drugs are legalized. According to one study, 17 percent of state prisoners and 18 percent of federal prisoners committed their first crimes in order to obtain money to buy illegal drugs.[19] With free or low-cost drugs available at local clinics, addicts would no longer need to resort to crime to support their addictions.

Finally, I know that making such a momentous change in our national approach to our drug abuse problem will be much more complex than I have presented here. So I have two specific suggestions for getting started.

First, challenge the nation's graduate schools of business to develop plans to put the illegal drug industry out of business in the United States. If those schools are teaching our brightest future

---

[19] Source: "Financial Cost of the War on Drugs" by Christina Gleason, May 6, 2008

business leaders how to create and run successful businesses, they should be a gold mine of ideas for driving the drug cartels into bankruptcy in the United States.

Second, put our schools of public health to work on developing a system for making the heretofore illegal drugs of abuse available legally nationwide and for developing programs for offering a nationwide network of treatment centers for addicts who want to overcome their addiction.

That will get us started. And if we can follow through on all of this, I believe we have a really good chance of bringing an end to 90 percent or more of the illegal drug trade in this country.

Is this a perfect solution? Absolutely not.

There will always be young people who try to work around the edges of legalized drugs and who will experiment with fringe drugs, just as today there are young people who manage to start smoking cigarettes before they can buy them legally, or who experiment with alcohol – sometimes to excess – before they can purchase it legally.

If, however, we can take the profit out of the mainstream illegal drugs of abuse, we can put the huge marketing force of today's drug pushers out of work and bring an end to the enormous economic pressures that are pushing drugs into our local communities and into the hands of our young people.

Alternatively, if we keep on doing what we've been doing for the past 30 years, nothing will change – except, possibly, to get worse.

Energy – Part I

9

In the United States, we're like surfers. We ride waves. Waves of fashion. Waves of technology. Waves of fads.

Our approach to energy conservation is no exception. In attempting to reduce our dependence on fossil fuels and to reduce greenhouse gas emissions, we're riding the wave of electric vehicles and hybrids. Even the fad of bio-fuels. The only problem is that these technologies are at best only partial answers in the long term and will have little effect in the short term. Moreover, they may carry long-term costs that are largely being ignored.

There are, however, several common-sense approaches to reducing our consumption of fossil fuels, all of which would have significant impact in the near future and help us buy time for development of entirely different systems that, in the long term, will greatly reduce our use of fossil fuels – in some instances, eliminate them completely.

The most obvious involves gasoline requirements for our cars and light trucks. Another involves movement of freight. Still another involves our use of "labor-saving" devices such as leaf blowers.

Let's look first at our approach to the use of petroleum-based products to fuel our standard motor vehicles – cars and trucks. There is good reason to consider this first. According to the U.S. Department of Energy's July 2012 edition of the Transportation Energy Data Book, cars and trucks account for some 57 percent of our national consumption of petroleum.[20] What that means is that if we want to reduce our consumption of petroleum, we have the greatest leverage by reducing the amount of fuel consumed by cars and trucks.

That's why, for example, Congress in its wisdom keeps increasing the "miles per gallon" requirement for the fleet average. What this means, of course, is that each automaker must produce a mix of vehicles that on average will achieve a certain minimum miles per gallon.

That is to say, for example, that the Ford Motor Company's mix of automobiles must, on average, achieve the mandated minimum miles per gallon as measured in tests by the federal government. And the fact is that the greater fuel efficiency of our new cars is having a beneficial impact on our consumption of crude oil.

At the same time, however, our drivers speed merrily away on the nation's highways and back roads, ignoring speed limits, wasting energy every mile they drive, and making a mockery of the government-mandated mileage requirements, which are measured for highway driving at 55 mph. And, we've done nothing to change that.

If we were really interested in reducing our consumption of crude oil, we would take two steps that would have rapid impact.

First, we could cut our oil consumption dramatically simply by banning the sale of cars and light trucks using gasoline engines, replacing those engines with light-weight, cleaning-burning diesel engines or with so-called flex-fuel engines (engines capable of burning

---

[20] Transportation Energy Data Book: Edition 31, July 2012. Prepared by Oak Ridge National Laboratory for the U.S. Department of Energy.

gasoline-alcohol blends containing up to 85 percent alcohol) in all new cars sold in this country – say by the 2020 model year. We could do the same thing for boats that have inboard engines.

Such a deadline would provide ample time for automakers to prepare for the changeover. It would also provide time for refining companies and the retail gasoline station industry to transition to a diesel and flex-fuel economy while continuing to serve the pre-existing need for conventional gasoline, much as was accomplished when the sale of leaded gasoline was phased out.

Sound radical? Well, perhaps it is. But consider for the moment what replacing gasoline with diesel as the major fuel for cars, light trucks and boats would accomplish.

Diesel engines are much more-fuel efficient than gasoline engines. Moreover, nearly every measure of the difference in fuel economy I've read suggests that diesel-powered automobiles get 20 percent or more miles per gallon than identical car models powered by gasoline engines.

Imagine how much less oil we would consume if our automobiles and light trucks consumed 20 percent less fuel.

I'm not arguing that we should stop work on electric cars and hybrid power trains. They have a place. In many parts of the country, drivers travel only a few miles on any single trip. For those drivers, electric cars make perfect sense. But, as anyone who travels outside of our major metropolitan areas knows, there are millions of Americans for whom electric cars make no sense at all – at least, not with current technology.

For example, we have two cars – a minivan and a compact. We live 45 miles from the nearest city or large town. A single day of running errands in town involves driving well over 100 miles – often as much as 150 miles or more. For us, clean-burning diesel cars would make perfect sense.

Hybrid cars might also make sense if consumers could justify the higher cost of those cars on the grounds of the money they'd save in fuel consumption. But they can't – not until the cost of the hybrids comes closer to the cost of same size conventional cars. It takes too long for the lower fuel costs resulting from the improved gas mileage to offset the difference in price for many consumers to make that larger investment with the higher monthly payments.

There is a second action we as a country could take that would have even more immediate impact on our consumption of oil for automobiles and trucks, both gasoline and diesel. We could enforce our speed limits – aggressively!

You laugh? Well, let me confess. I'm a reformed speeder. I saw the light when the price of regular gasoline first hit $3.50 per gallon. My reformation had an immediate impact. Yes, it took a little longer to get to our destination. But our average highway gas mileage for the minivan we owned at that time went from about 20 miles per gallon (mpg) to between 24 and 25 mpg. Moreover, through a combination of driving the speed limit and driving the van more gently (i.e., less aggressively) on urban and suburban roads, our average miles per gallon per tank including both highway and city driving increased by a similar percentage – on both cars! As a result, our gasoline bill was reduced by about 20 percent.

More recently, driving a newer car equipped with a digital readout of average miles per gallon, I have confirmed that driving at the posted speed limits instead of 10 mph above the speed limit results in a 20 percent or greater increase in our gas mileage (See Table 5).

Think about it. When the price of gasoline is $3.50 per gallon, improving our mileage by 20 percent is like getting a discount of 70 cents per gallon of gasoline! When the price gets up to $4.00 per gallon, the savings is equivalent to 80 cents per gallon. That's a savings of from $12 to $15 every time I fill the minivan's tank when gas is at $4 per gallon. That's why I'm a reformed speeder.

Table 5
Automobile Fuel Economy at Different Speeds

Speed	Miles per gallon	% change in MPG
75 mpg	22.2 mpg	n/a
65 mpg	27.0 mpg	+21.6%
	* * *	
70 mpg	24.6 mpg	n/a
60 mpg	30.2 mpg	+21.7%
	* * *	
65 mpg	27.0 mpg	n/a
55 mpg	32.6 mpg	+20.7%

Note: These measurements were made on Interstate 95 in South Florida while driving a 2009 Toyota Sienna minivan. Measurements were made using the car's digital readout of average MPG over test runs of 25 or more miles with the car speed controlled electronically by the cruise control feature.

* * *

Think about it also in terms of our national consumption of crude oil. If enforcing speed limits reduced our national fuel consumption by only 10 percent, the result would be an immediate reduction of more than 5 percent in our overall consumption of crude oil.

So, how can we get everyone to reform?

Actually, I think it would be relatively easy to do using the carrot and stick approach. You make it rewarding (the carrot) to obey the speed limits by widely publicizing how much money drivers can save by getting better gas mileage; and you make it painful to speed (the stick) by pointing out the cost in time and money when you get stopped for speeding – time sitting on the side of the road while the policeman runs your tags through the computer and writes up your ticket, and money spent when paying the ticket – not to mention the likely increase in insurance premiums as points are added to your driving record.

But there's a problem.

Today, police usually do not stop people for speeding unless they are driving more than 10 mph over the speed limit. A case in point: According to news reports about speed-enforcement cameras installed in various states and localities, such cameras are triggered only when a vehicle is traveling more than 10 mph over the speed limit.

I suspect this practice is the result of too many lawyers getting cases dismissed or getting their clients found "not guilty" by raising doubts about the accuracy of speed-detection devices.

But what do you think would happen if (1) laws were changed in every state so that no points were placed against drivers licenses unless the drivers were caught going more than 10 miles per hour over the speed limit; (2) speed detection devices were required to be tested and calibrated on a regular schedule so that their accuracy was certifiable; (3) the use of speed cameras was greatly increased so that they became commonplace; and (4), law-enforcement officials began ticketing people for going more than 5 mph over the speed limit (except when passing another vehicle on a two-lane road)?

In this situation, people driving more than 5 mph over the speed limit would have a choice between paying the fine (it should be a graduated fine whose severity is related to the speed of the offender and the frequency with which the person is caught speeding) or going to traffic court, which, of course, costs both time and money.

And what would happen if we were to greatly increase the use of speed cameras programmed to catch cars going more than 5 mph over the speed limit? Initially, tickets could be advisory. "The driver of your car was caught exceeding the speed limit. Speeding wastes gasoline and our nation is working diligently to reduce our consumption of petroleum-based fuels. To encourage drivers to obey our speed limits, we have installed numerous speed cameras and will begin enforcing speed limits using these cameras. Speeding will cost you money, not only because you will use more gasoline, but also because you will be ticketed and fined." Or words to that effect.

Yes, many speeders initially might be unhappy, but with an active public relations campaign accompanying the issuance first of advisory tickets and subsequently of real tickets, America's drivers would soon begin to get the message. Under these circumstances, I believe most drivers would become much better about obeying speed limits and, as a result, our national consumption of gasoline and diesel fuel would be significantly reduced.

One note: I have found it ironic that many drivers argue against speed cameras because "the only reason they have them is so they can make money." They never even acknowledge than the driver of their car was breaking the law. In their view, the city or state is at fault for using unfair technology to catch them. In their view, speeders are never at fault. There is something wrong here.

A second note: I am aware that some jurisdictions have had trouble with their speed camera contractors sending out bogus tickets to make more money. The laws allowing the use of speed cameras should be written to make it a felony offense to send out bogus speeding tickets and hold the officers and/or owners of any company found sending out bogus tickets criminally responsible.

Five more observations concerning fuel economy and cars:

First, all cars and light trucks should be equipped with cruise control. Cruise control helps drivers obey the speed limit.

Second, all cars and light trucks should be equipped with prominent displays providing real-time information about the miles per gallon the car is getting. These displays are already standard on many cars. Frankly, they should be standard on every car and truck sold in this country. This kind of instant feedback would help drivers learn how to drive for maximum fuel economy, thereby reducing our consumption of gasoline and diesel fuel.

Third, we should modify existing driver-education programs to teach driving for maximum fuel economy right alongside driving safety. I'm not going to list them here, but there are several good driving and car maintenance habits that contribute to better gas mileage. Unfortunately, we do not now emphasize them in our driver-education programs. Let's change that.

Fourth, a question: Why do we need cars with such large engines that they can accelerate from 0 to 60 in four or five seconds? Or that can be driven at speeds well in excess of 100 mph when there is no highway in the country where one can drive at those speeds legally?

I know that it would be politically difficult to mandate an upper limit on automobile engine horsepower. But if we can't do that –

although we should try to do it – it should at least be possible to make it very expensive to drive such a car by imposing an annual tax on cars or light trucks with excessively powerful engines. And yes, I said an *annual* tax.

I realize that strong objections to such a proposal will emerge from some quarters. If, however, it is in the national interest to reduce our consumption of oil and to reduce our emissions of greenhouse gases, then "We the People" through our elected representatives have the right to place limits on such things as engine size. Alternatively, we have the right through our elected representatives to make it very costly for individuals who choose to thumb their noses at our national goals by driving so-called muscle cars or trucks. And we should do so.

Fifth, insofar as the highest legal speed limit in this country is 80 mph, why don't we mandate electronic speed governors so that cars (other than vehicles used for law enforcement) cannot be driven faster than 80 mph? This could be done easily and, if the governor were part of the car's built-in computer, it could not be easily by-passed or disconnected.

Now, to trucks – excluding light trucks.

First, the American Trucking Association recommends enacting a national maximum speed limit of 65 mph. The association also recommends the mandatory installation of speed governors on trucks manufactured after 1992 so that they could not be driven faster than 65 mph.

Although the trucking association's recommendation for a national speed limit includes both cars and trucks, it is probably not possible politically to return to a national speed limit for cars. For that reason, I do not suggest attempting that. However, I do support a national speed limit for trucks for both reasons of safety and energy conservation. According to the website *trucksdeliver.org*, "a truck traveling at 75 mph consumes 27 percent more fuel than one going at 65 mph." Reducing highway speed limits for trucks to a maximum of 65 mph would, they report, save 2.8 million gallons of diesel fuel in 10 years. Extending that national speed limit to buses would provide even greater savings.

Finally, we should also require that all large trucks and buses be equipped with "Electronic On-Board Recorders" (EOBRs) that require truck drivers to identify themselves before starting the engine and then record the driver's speed as well as the hours driven. This type of EOBR is already mandated in Europe. At this writing, there have been on-again and off-again proposals in this country to require commercial trucks and buses to have EOBRs that identify the drivers and record the hours driven to enable enforcement of laws limiting the number of hours per day drivers are permitted to drive, but EOBRs are not yet mandated by law. The owners of some private truck fleets, however, are using these devices to help them manage their trucks more effectively.

Common sense also suggests, however, that we should follow Europe's lead and use EOBRs to record speed as well as hours driven, with the information on both available to law enforcement if the truck is stopped for a violation.

I would also make EOBRs mandatory on all government-owned vehicles and available as optional equipment on privately-owned fleet automobiles and light trucks as well as on personal automobiles and light trucks. In this way, supervisors could make random checks of the EOBRs to ensure that employees are obeying speed laws. I, for one, have often been passed by people driving state-owned cars who are wasting my tax dollars on gasoline by driving over the speed limit.

Let me turn now to the movement of freight.

Over the past 20 or more years, Congress has greatly reduced funds available to the Army Corps of Engineers to dredge the Intracoastal Waterway (ICW), which runs along the East Coast from the Chesapeake Bay to the Florida Keys. The popular explanation is that the federal government shouldn't waste taxpayer money dredging a waterway for owners of private yachts who want to cruise to Florida for the winter.

But this explanation ignores one vital point. The most important function of the ICW is its use by commercial barge traffic to move freight, including or perhaps most importantly, petroleum products. Some years ago, I read an estimate that, if all of the freight moved by barges up and down the East Coast using the ICW were instead moved by truck because the ICW became unusable, we'd have to build a second interstate highway parallel to I-95 along the East Coast to accommodate the added truck traffic. While I can't vouch for the accuracy of the claim, the very words make an important point: If barges don't carry it, trucks will – and much less efficiently in terms of fuel consumption.

Moreover, those barges coming up from the South don't stop once they reach the Chesapeake Bay. From there they can easily continue to Philadelphia, New York and Boston.

Tugs can move barges with much more fuel efficiency than trucks can move the same cargoes, but the failure to maintain the ICW has resulted in severe shoaling in some parts of the waterway and continues to threaten its viability.

Freight also moves on railroads with much less expenditure of fuel. Money spent on railroad infrastructure would pay enormous benefits in fuel savings and our federal government should be finding ways to encourage increased use of rail to move freight. High speed passenger service may be more glamorous and does have benefits as an alternative to travel by automobile, but increasing the use of rail to move freight would also pay enormous benefits in terms of transportation efficiency.

There is one other widespread use of gasoline that needs a good look – that is, the use of gasoline to power millions of leaf blowers, weed whackers, etc. used for lawn care and general lawn maintenance and to clean patios, porches, sidewalks, driveways, parking lots and, even, city streets.

The questions I have are these: Why do we need to use gasoline-powered blowers to clean grass clippings from sidewalks and driveways or autumn leaves from lawns, sidewalk and driveways? Why, too, do we need gasoline-powered devices to trim grass along the edges of sidewalks and driveways? And, why do we need gasoline-powered weed whackers to cut weeds? We did without such devices for many, many years. Lawn rakes work just fine for cleaning up leaves. Brooms work for sweeping grass clippings or leaves from sidewalks and driveways. I grew up using a manual edger to trim the grass along my parents' driveway. And I still use a long-handled weed cutter that I swing back and forth to cut back large weeds or small brush.

While it is true that individually these devices use only a small amount of gasoline, it is also true that collectively they consume hundreds of thousands if not millions of gallons of gasoline each year. One can argue that they are easier to use and perhaps more efficient than manual alternatives. But the price we pay for that ease of use and small increase in efficiency is a large and unnecessary expenditure of gasoline.

Common sense has made me question the widespread use of these devices for several years, particularly as I've seen workers using blowers to clean leaves and grass clippings from sidewalks onto city and suburban streets and then watched other workers use similar blowers to clean the leaves and grass clippings from the streets.

Today, with the importance of reducing both our consumption of carbon-based fuels and our importation of oil and gasoline, I believe it is time to rethink the use of these gasoline-powered blowers, trimmers and weed whackers.

So there's my list of common-sense ways to reduce our consumption of petroleum-based fuels. Aggressively enforcing speed limits and enacting a national speed limit of 65 mph for large trucks would have an immediate impact on our consumption of these fuels. Setting a date to phase out gasoline powered cars, light trucks and inboard-motor boats, and replacing them with diesel powered vehicles, would have another large impact on our consumption of these fuels, beginning four or five years from the time the decision was made.

Other suggestions – for example, teaching driving for fuel economy in driver education programs, enacting a national speed limit for large trucks, placing speed governors on cars and trucks, requiring electronic on-board recorders on trucks and all fleet vehicles – will help ensure that people drive for maximum fuel economy.

In the longer term, increasing bulk transportation by water along our East and Gulf Coasts and increasing use of rail transportation for long distance freight hauling will further reduce our national consumption of petroleum products. And, finally, devising ways to greatly reduce the use of gasoline-powered yard tools such as weed whackers and leaf blowers will further reduce our consumption of gasoline. Even more important, it will underscore the importance that we as a nation place on conservation of fossil fuels and reduction in our emissions of greenhouse gases.

Energy – Part II

10

There is a second side to the energy equation – our consumption of fossil fuels to satisfy our almost insatiable demand for electricity.

To begin, we may – repeat "may" – be doing better when it comes to reducing our dependence on fossil fuels to provide the electricity our country requires. But here, too, we are captured by what is popular in the moment. Moreover, we are so focused on moving away from fossil fuels for the large-scale generation of electricity that little thought is given to common-sense approaches to reducing the demand side. And, finally, we're ignoring the Law of Unintended Consequences.

Let me be specific.

What are the two largest draws on energy in every home in the country? One is heating and/or cooling. The other is providing hot water.

First, heating and cooling.

Common sense suggests that we develop a *national* building code related to energy conservation for both residential and commercial structures.

Now, before anyone automatically rebels against such an intrusion of the federal government on local prerogatives, consider the following: In reality if not in name, we already have a national building code for new homes built in flood and hurricane zones. If those homes are not built according to code requirements established by the Federal Energy Management Administration (FEMA), building inspectors will not approve the construction, the owners will not be able to obtain mortgages, and the structures even if built will not be eligible for flood insurance. While this may not be a national building code written into the national law, these FEMA requirements are a de facto federal building code and there is no reason we could not have similar requirements relating to energy efficiency for private and commercial structures.

What do I have in mind? Consider this: When our house was built, our contractor suggested we use 2x6 studs in our exterior walls rather than 2x4 studs so that we could have six inches of insulation instead of the usual four inches. He assured me the cost savings to heat and cool our house would more than pay for the extra cost of the larger studs.

So, why not make six-inch exterior walls and six inches of insulation in exterior walls part of a national building code for residential housing? And for commercial housing such as motels and hotels as well? Why not a national building code requirement for double-paned windows? Or a national code stipulating a minimum thickness of insulation in attics. Or, the use of storm doors year-round to reduce heat loss through exterior doors. These are requirements that could be put in place quickly and take effect immediately.

Yes, such requirements would add to the cost of construction but – and this is important – *the incremental cost would be small.*

In building our house, for example, using 2x6 studs in the exterior walls added less than one quarter of one percent to the cost of the house. There was also a slightly increased cost for the thicker insulation and a larger but still small increased cost of the double-paned windows, but these incremental costs were all miniscule next to the total cost of the house. More importantly, there can be no question that we have enjoyed lower energy bills for heating and cooling as a result.

Now, let's look at the other major source of energy consumption in our homes – our hot-water heaters.

We waste enormous amounts of energy keeping tanks of hot water heated to 110 or, more likely, 120 degrees Fahrenheit 24 hours a day, seven days a week when we use hot water only intermittently. In fact, by some estimates, between 14 and 25 percent of the energy consumed in our homes can be attributed to our hot water heaters.

So think about how much energy could be saved in each household if all of us had water heaters that produced hot water only when we were actually using it. And then think about reducing your electric bill by 5 or 10 percent or more.

This is not rocket science. Nor do we need new technologies.

In 1955 – that's right, nearly 60 years ago as I write these words – I stayed in a youth hostel in Vienna, Austria, that had an instantaneous hot water heater in a large shower room with multiple shower heads. It was right there on the wall and, when we turned on the hot water to take our showers, the water heater was turned on.

The point of this observation is simple. Instantaneous water heaters and the technology for them have been around for decades. We just haven't adopted it in this country.

But what do you think would happen if a national building code required instantaneous water heaters in all new residential construction beginning January 1, 2016 and Congress or a federal agency mandated that only instantaneous hot water heaters be sold in the United States after December 31, 2020, for use in residential buildings? First, all new home construction would have energy-saving water heaters. Second, the 2020 date for ending the sale of tank-style water heaters would allow time to phase-out the tank-style hot water heaters and for all manufacturers to phase in their own brands of instantaneous heaters. The phase-out of tank-style heaters would mean that every older home, apartment, and condominium needing to replace water heaters would have to replace the energy-wasting tank-style heaters with an energy-saving instantaneous heater. Today, the most efficient instantaneous water heaters use gas – natural gas or propane. For people whose homes are heated with baseboard hot water or radiators, the furnaces can be converted to provide instantaneous hot-water systems. In fact, we installed such a system in one of our previous homes in the 1970s when we had to replace our old oil-burning furnace and changed from a hot-air heating system to baseboard hot-water heat. The old tank-style water heater went out with the old furnace.

There are instantaneous electric water heaters, but they need improvement. If, however, tank-style water heaters were removed from the marketplace, I have no doubt that more efficient electric water heaters meeting the energy-savings standards in the national building code would be developed. Equally important, as the market for instantaneous water heaters became exponentially larger, the cost of all such water heaters would come down as the market size and competition increased.

But let's not think only in terms of private homes and apartments. I have stayed in motels where I've had to let the water run through the hot water spigot for two or three minutes or longer before getting hot water. Think not only about how much hot water is being wasted in those pipes because the hot water tank was so far from our room, but also about how much water was simply being run down the drain and wasted.

That is why I've suggested applying this code change broadly to residential construction, including hotels and motels.

Obviously, commercial buildings have different hot-water needs than do private homes. But what would happen if our new national building code required motels and hotels built after that same future date – e.g. 2020 – to have instantaneous hot water systems, if not for individual rooms, then perhaps for each floor, or each group of ten rooms? I am not an engineer, so I cannot prescribe how such a code should be written. There are, however, plenty of engineers out there who could easily figure out how such a building code should be structured to make it practical and effective in reducing energy consumption for providing hot water in hotels and motels. Then, instead of maintaining very large tanks of hot water 24 hours a day to meet the morning shower needs of 25 or 50 or even 100 rooms, a series of more efficient instantaneous hot-water heaters would do the job.

Those are some common-sense suggestions on the energy consumption side. Let's turn now to the energy-production side of the issue.

First, bio fuels – e.g., alcohol for blending with gasoline to power flex-fuel cars, trucks and boats.

If my suggestion to replace gasoline powered engines in cars, trucks and inboard-motor boats with diesel engines is adopted, production of gasoline will be greatly reduced and alcohol blends with gasoline possibly would gradually disappear. If that suggestion is not taken, however, alcohol blends with gasoline could become a major tactic for reducing our consumption of petroleum. In that case, we need to rethink our approach to production of biofuels.

The effort in the United States to produce alcohol for gasoline has been centered primarily on the use of corn as the raw material for production of alcohol. Frankly, this has been absurd – not because we shouldn't try to develop alcohol as a fuel for cars, but because of the focus on corn as the raw material.

In a world in which starvation remains a serious problem, it makes no sense at all to use a primary food crop (whether for livestock or people) as a raw material for production of alcohol.

The technology might be easier and the supply handily nearby, but there are other plants that could be used as the raw material for alcohol production without putting pressure on the price and supply of foodstuffs. Switch grass, which is often mentioned, has the advantage that you don't have to replant it every year. Moreover, I'm sure there are other perennial plants that could be used. For example, has anyone considered kudzu, a leafy vine that grows aggressively and is nearly impossible to kill?

The point is this: To the extent that alcohol can be used as a replacement for petroleum-based automotive fuel, we should produce that alcohol from plant raw materials other than primary food crops. Moreover, we should avoid taking land away from the production of food crops to grow raw materials for alcohol because that too would put pressure on food prices.

Some people may be tempted to argue that the automobile industry would need many years to develop cars that will run on alcohol, but they would be wrong. The auto industry – including Ford and General Motors – has been selling cars that run on alcohol in Brazil for many years. Some run on 100 percent alcohol, but most sold now are engineered to run on gasoline with a relatively high-ethanol (alcohol) content. In fact, Ford, Chevrolet, Toyota, Nissan, Mitsubishi, Peugeot, Renault and Citroen now all sell flexible-fuel cars in Brazil that can use almost any blend of alcohol and gasoline. In fact, in 2009, some 94 percent of all cars sold in Brazil were these "flex-fuel" cars.

In the United States, at least one of the auto companies (Ford) is selling flex-fuel cars that will run on both regular gasoline and an E85 fuel that is 85 percent alcohol and 15 percent gasoline. Most of these cars have been sold in the Midwest because that is where much of our ethanol production (from corn) is centered and where the E85 fuel is more readily available.

Over the past two or three years, however, I have been seeing many more flex-fuel cars in our local area – Charleston, S.C. – and we are even seeing E85 gas pumps at local gas stations. What this means, of course, is that flex-fuel cars and E85 fuel are become more widely available. Frankly, for the automotive market, I suspect that the long-term answer to petroleum-based fuel will be the use of hydrogen as the automotive fuel of choice. That, however, will require significant research and development, particularly in the area of infrastructure to provide "hydrogen stations" where we now have gasoline stations.

There will also have to be a hard look at the energy costs of producing hydrogen. It will do little good to create a hydrogen-based automobile industry if the energy required to produce the hydrogen fuel is disproportionately large. So I suggest the following: 1) That we examine the energy cost of producing hydrogen before making a commitment to a hydrogen-based automobile industry; and 2) that we try to anticipate the potential "unintended consequences" before taking steps we might later regret.

Switching gears…

Another important action with little downside risk on the energy production side would be to make it more attractive for individual homeowners and businesses to produce a portion of their own electricity using solar panels, wind turbines or water turbines.

A minimum of three enabling steps would be required: One is a permanent tax credit and depreciation allowance for anyone – private citizen or business entity – willing to invest in solar panels, wind turbines or water turbines to produce his own electricity rather than relying totally on the public electrical grid. The tax credit – which could be taken against taxes owed or be partially or totally refunded by government if a taxpayer's income in that year is such that his tax bill is less than the tax credit – would provide an initial financial incentive for individual homeowners and businesses to make such an investment. The depreciation allowance – which should be structured so that unused portions can be passed from owner to owner – would then provide a longer-term incentive.

The second step would be passage of a law to require all electric utilities to install so-called "smart meters" for customers who install such energy-producing equipment. The smart meters would enable homeowners and businesses to feed their excess electrical energy production into the electrical grid and to receive credit for that excess power. If electric utilities were required to provide such two-way electric meters wherever businesses or homeowners were installing non-carbon-based electric generating-capacity, then homeowners or businesses willing to invest in wind turbines, solar panels or water turbines to generate electricity would be able to receive credit on their electric bills for any energy they fed into the grid.

The third step is a federal law that would specifically exempt electricity-generating wind turbines and solar panels used to generate electricity from state or local zoning regulations and from deed restrictions or neighborhood restrictive covenants that might otherwise block the installation of these devices. Without such a nationwide law, years would be required to bring about the changes required in local communities to allow wind turbines and solar panels to "mar" the landscape.

In time, the combination of the suggested tax incentives, the energy credit from the power companies as a result of the two-way meter, and the reduction in a homeowner's or business owner's purchase of electricity from the local utility would pay for the costs of installing their own electricity-generating capacity. In some parts of the country, this could have significant impact on the consumption of coal, oil and natural gas for the production of electricity.

Finally, as suggested earlier, in whatever measures we adopt to increase our energy efficiency and reduce our consumption of fossil fuels, we must do a better job of recognizing the consequences – particularly the unintended negative consequences – of our decisions. In particular, I am thinking of how we are going to dispose of millions of compact fluorescent light (CFL) bulbs, all of which contain mercury that can poison our land, waterways, groundwater and bodies if they are broken or disposed of incorrectly.

In the rush to persuade the public to use CFL bulbs to save energy and reduce electric bills, I am concerned that little thought has been given to this question and that even less planning has gone into solving what are potentially major disposal, environmental and public health problems. Theoretically, legislation passed in 2007 will result in the phasing out of 40-, 60-, 75- or 100- watt incandescent light bulbs in this country with the expectation that CFL bulbs will replace them, although at this writing Congress has blocked the prohibition of their sale, which was to have gone into effect January 1, 2014.

From the perspective of energy conservation, the legislation made sense. CFL bulbs use only about 25 percent of the electricity consumed by incandescent bulbs. From an environmental viewpoint, however, I'm not convinced. Consider the recommendations from the U.S. Environmental Protection Agency in Table 7 for what consumers should do if they break a compact fluorescent light bulb:

Table 7

Before Cleanup

1. Have people and pets leave the room and avoid the breakage on the way out.
2. Open a window or door to the outdoors and leave the room for 5 to 10 minutes.
3. Shut off the central forced-air heating/air conditioning (H&AC) system, if you have one.
4. Collect the materials you will need to clean up the broken bulb:

- *Stiff cardboard or paper*
- *Sticky tape (e.g. duct tape)*
- *Damp paper towel or disposable wet wipes (for hard surface)*
- *Glass jar with a metal lid (such as a canning jar) or a sealable plastic bag(s)*

Cleanup Steps for Hard Surface

1. *Carefully scoop up glass fragments and powder using stiff paper or cardboard and place debris and paper/cardboard in a glass container with a metal lid. If a glass jar is not*

available, use a sealable plastic bag. (NOTE: Since a plastic bag will not prevent mercury vapor from escaping, remove the plastic bag from the home after cleanup.)

2. Use sticky tape to pick up any remaining small glass fragments and powder. Place used tape in the glass jar or plastic bag.
3. Wipe the area clean with damp paper towels or disposable wet wipes. Place towels/wipes in glass jar or plastic bag.
4. Vacuuming hard surface during cleanup is not recommended unless broken glass remains after all other cleanup steps have been taken. (NOTE: It is possible that vacuuming could spread mercury-containing powder or mercury vapor, although information on this problem is limited.) If vacuuming is needed to ensure removal of all broken glass, keep the following tips in mind:

- *Keep a window or door to the outside open.*
- *Vacuum the area where the bulb was broken using vacuum hose, if available; and,*
- *Remove the vacuum bag (or empty and wipe the canister) and seal the bag/vacuum debris and any materials used to clean the vacuum in a plastic bag.*

5. Promptly place all bulb debris and cleanup materials, including the vacuum cleaner bags, outdoors in a trash container or protected area until the materials can be disposed of properly.

- *Check with your local or state government about disposal requirements in your area. Some states and communities require fluorescent bulbs (broken or unbroken) to be taken to a local recycling center.*

6. Wash your hands with soap and water after disposing of the

jars or plastic bags containing bulb debris and cleanup materials.

7. Continue to air out the room where the bulb was broken and leave the H&AC system shut off, as practical, for several hours.

NOTE: Equally detailed instructions are provided for cleaning up a broken fluorescent bulb on carpets or rugs.
Source: www.epa.gov/cfl/cflcleanup-detailed.html

* * *

My questions are these: (1) Did Congress consider the health implications of millions of CFL bulbs in use throughout the country in homes and public places such as in table lamps in restaurants and the health risks to consumers when one of those bulbs is broken? (2) Did Congress consider the problem of disposing of these millions of CFL bulbs and the environmental impact of the inevitable improper disposal by a public that either doesn't know about the hazard or is too lazy to dispose of them properly? And (3) might we not be better advised to reverse the CFL mandate allowing incandescent bulbs back on the market, banning CFL bulbs, and mandating the use of LED (light-emitting diode) lights in their place as soon as production of LED bulbs can be ramped up to meet the need? LED lights are more broadly available than just two or three years ago and their price is coming down. Also, even though their initial purchase price is high, they have an approximate lifetime of 30 years – five or six times the life expectancy for CFLs – so that any higher initial costs would be more than offset by their long life span.

My point is this: Our lawmakers need to take into consideration the long-term consequences of any legislation mandating the use of new products. I can see similar disposal problems arising, for example, as we begin to have large numbers of electric cars on our roads, each of them with multiple batteries that must be disposed of at some time.

Has anyone stopped to think about that potential problem? Common sense tells me that this, too, should be thought out and planned for ahead of time – before we suddenly have millions of batteries from electric cars that need to be disposed of. Or, perhaps, what we need is development of a technology to recycle those batteries so that worn-out batteries can be "reborn" and then reused.

Finally, if a decision is made to increase the use of nuclear power to provide electricity to our national grid, that decision must be accompanied by implementation of a realistic plan for disposing of nuclear waste. Because of the problem of NMBY (not in my back yard) we do not yet have a long-term plan for disposing of the nuclear waste we have already produced. It would be folly to start building new nuclear-generating plants without simultaneously providing for the long-term disposal of our nuclear wastes.

In summary, there is much we can do relatively easily and quickly to reduce our consumption of petroleum-based fuels significantly. Many of these fuel-saving ideas are just plain common sense. Yes, they may require changing our mindset about some things – for example, as discussed in Chapter 9, about how we drive and how fast our cars can go. They may also require that we implement national standards in areas of energy efficiency in residential and commercial buildings, and limited changes in the regulation of electric utilities to encourage more widespread use of newer generating systems. And they most certainly will require us to think through all of these energy-saving ideas so that we minimize possible unintended and undesirable consequences of our decisions.

But there is much we can do quickly and with little downside risk. All we really need is the public willingness to get on with the job.

Politics Gone Awry

11

Political practices have changed dramatically since the U.S. Congress was created more than 200 years ago. At that time, men viewed their election to Congress as a term of public service. Today, men and women elected to Congress are often embarking on what they hope will be a career spanning decades. In fact, I wonder what language delegates to the Constitutional Convention might have added to the provisions of the Constitution establishing the House and Senate if they had foreseen the possibility of people making such elected offices a decades-long career rather than a short term of public service.

In the past 40 years, however, one particular change has emerged in our political landscape and in Congress that brings into question the ability of our democracy to function: that is, the rise of extreme political partisanship.

The problem, of course, is that often the ideas of the far left and of the far right are not necessarily best for the country no matter how strongly liberals or conservatives believe in them. Almost always, what is best for the country is found in the middle – somewhere between the ideas espoused by liberals and conservatives. And that is why we must restore a spirit of cooperation and willingness to compromise in the halls of Congress.

In our political arena today, however, it has reached the point at which ideology and conformity to that ideology have replaced getting things done to help move the country forward. Among Republicans, more conservative members of the party are challenging sitting Republicans in primaries because the sitting members are not perceived as sufficiently conservative. In fact, many on the right have become so convinced of the truth of their political belief system that they follow it with a religious fervor. It is no accident that many of those on the political right who are most fervently partisan in their politics are also among the most fervent in their religious views.

Those on the right, of course, blame the partisanship on the left. And almost certainly, both sides of the aisle have contributed to the present situation. But with the exception of blocking a nomination or two to the U.S. Supreme Court, I do not think it is truthful to blame liberals for the current situation.

I trace the beginning of this development to the 1964 candidacy for president of conservative Republican Barry Goldwater – a campaign with which I had direct experience. In my political memory, which begins in 1948, Goldwater was the first politically strong conservative candidate to receive his party's nomination. I had followed the Republican primary campaigns in 1964 and was able to attend the GOP National Convention in San Francisco when Goldwater received his party's nomination. And the experience frightened me. Literally.

Let me explain. At the time, I was a 26-year-old graduate student studying journalism. For the record, I was also a registered Republican and had voted for Richard Nixon in the 1960 election. I had attempted to obtain press credentials as an editor of my university newspaper and as a correspondent for a local radio station, but my application was turned down by the National Republican party. (I did, on the other hand, receive press credentials for the Democratic National Convention that same year.)

However, I had been covering the Iowa caucuses and state convention in my role as a reporter for our university newspaper during the spring semester and had come to know the head of the state Republican Party. When I presented my problem to him, he appointed me an assistant sergeant at arms for the state delegation. That's how I was able to attend the GOP National Convention.

My first memory upon arriving on the grounds of San Francisco's Cow Palace, where the convention was held, is of a bookstand where a man was selling a variety of "conservative" literature. Looking at the selection, I saw prominently displayed the worst racist hate literature I had seen in my life – a book which, to me, defined the word "obscene." This, you will remember if you are old enough, was just weeks after three civil-rights workers – Michael Schwerner, James Chaney, and Andrew Goodman – were murdered in Mississippi.

I have three other distinct memories of that convention. First, in the early days of the convention, the news media were allowed down on the convention floor to interview various delegates and delegation leaders. Much of the coverage coming from those interviews was favorable to moderate candidates Bill Scranton and Nelson Rockefeller. Goldwater delegates seemed to receive less attention.

As the nomination day approached, however, suddenly all reporters were banned from the convention floor. That stunned me. I was able to continue with my interviewing on the floor because my credentials identified me as an assistant sergeant at arms. But no accredited reporters were allowed on the floor.

The second of those memories is of the evening that Nelson Rockefeller – again, a moderate candidate – was scheduled to speak to the convention. When Rockefeller took to the podium to speak, a roar of shouting erupted from the gallery. The audience in the gallery

– or, at least, a large segment of that audience – continued shouting loudly so that Rockefeller was unable to speak.

This shouting went on for what seemed like an eternity until Senator Everett Dirksen, the grand old man of the Republican Party, went up to the microphone and, as only he with his hoarse, stentorian voice could have done, called for SILENCE! Dirksen went onto say something to the effect that people didn't have to agree with what Rockefeller had to say, but in the United States of America, they did have to allow him the opportunity to speak. And, Rockefeller was then allowed to make his speech.

The third of those memories is short and sweet. Immediately after the vote had been taken and Goldwater had won the nomination, the press was once again allowed onto the floor of the convention.

I relate this experience because it probably represented the first modern major demonstration in America of ideology-based political expression and absolute intolerance for any viewpoint that strayed from that ideology.

Moreover, the selling of racist literature at the convention, the Goldwater supporters' efforts to limit media access to delegates until after their candidate had secured the nomination, and the extraordinarily rude shouting down of Rockefeller in an effort to prevent him from expressing his views – as I have said above, those experiences frightened me. And they led me to vote for a democratic candidate for the first time in my young life. Before then, I had voted for republican candidates.

What we are seeing today is a replication on a vastly larger scale of what I saw in San Francisco in 1964.

Let me provide one or two other experiences.

In my first job as a newspaper reporter, I would occasionally drop by the executive editor's office to chat. I don't remember anything about most of those conversations. But I do distinctly remember one comment he made. I didn't understand it at the time and, in fact, had forgotten about it for almost 30 years. In the fall political campaigns of 1996, however, that comment came rushing back to me. And I have since come to understand it in spades. He was talking about what I have since learned was the Goebbels Theory of "the big lie."

Almost verbatim, this is what he said: "You know, Goebbels (the Nazi propaganda chief in World War II) had it right. If you tell a big enough lie and keep repeating it over and over, people will begin to believe it."

Why did I recall this conversation in 1996? Here's the answer:

My wife and I had been out of the country for most of the previous four years and so had been away from American politics and television for most of that time. But upon our return in the summer of 1996, I began watching television news to bring myself up to date on national politics. It was, after all, an election year.

I quickly realized two things: (1) Republicans were all speaking from the same script; and (2) Democrats didn't have any script. I also realized that what I was hearing in many comments from Republicans was somewhat different from fact as I understood it. But they kept repeating the same so-called facts over and over and, before long, they were being accepted *and* being reported by the news media without question.

It quickly became obvious that Republicans were getting and taking advantage of some very good public-relations training, including how to field difficult questions. I know this because I worked in public relations for a number of years and, in fact, participated as a co-instructor in many training sessions to teach business people how to use television interviews to get their messages out no matter what questions were asked.

First point: The advantage of having everyone speak from the same script is that your message gets out on all news outlets no matter who is interviewed.

Second point: To field difficult questions, you begin by acknowledging the question, then quickly transition to one of your scripted key points – regardless of whether it has anything to do with the question.

Why is this technique important from a public relations view? The only reason politicians or corporate executives accept invitations to be interviewed is so that they can deliver the messages they want the public to hear. So, even if the interviewer has a different agenda (i.e., wants to ask questions on other subjects), the job of the people being interviewed is to make their key points. They get away with it because they begin by acknowledging the question before transitioning to one of their key points. And, too, they get away with it because reporters don't want to appear rude or overly aggressively by calling them on it.

The result in 1996 was that Republican congressional candidates as a group were well organized and able to present a very coherent message even if some facts were twisted. Democrats, on the other hand, were all over the place, each one delivering his own personal ideas. There was no obvious Party message.

We saw the Goebbels technique for persuading people to believe things that were either untrue or only partially true widely used during the Bush administration's run-up to the invasion of Iraq. Moreover, this same technique has been used by former Vice President Dick

Cheney in attempting to justify controversial policies related to interrogating and detaining terrorist suspects during the Bush administration, especially in his repeated assertions in the first years of the next president's term of office that the country was less safe than during the Bush years because we had abandoned practices and procedures that Chaney sanctioned (but which were clearly illegal).

More importantly, as he repeated this message over and over again, some people began to believe it – and not only his fellow conservatives, but even members of the media who started asking other politicians whether we were less safe than during the Bush administration. Merely by asking the question, these reporters gave credence to Cheney's claims.

Perhaps the most flagrant use of the Goebbels "big lie" technique came during the summer of 2009 by opponents of efforts to bring about sweeping changes in the nation's health insurance practices and to extend health insurance coverage to all Americans. The outright lies – or should I call them "misleading statements?" — that were repeated over and over about the reform proposals not only frightened millions of people – particularly, the elderly – but also led to craftily encouraged public anger displayed in public meeting after public meeting.

This is what I mean when I talk about "politics gone awry."

Another example of politics gone awry were public comments made by politicians and talk show hosts during the first year of the Obama administration to the effect that they wanted "Obama to fail."

Regardless of your political persuasion, I want you to think about those statements – hoping that the Obama administration would fail. Like it or not, at the time those comments were made, Obama was going to be the president of the United States for four years. And those people wanted him to fail during those four years.

Consider the implications of the president failing for those four years.

He took office in the midst of a major recession. If Obama failed in dealing with that recession the country likely would have fallen into a deep depression rivaling that of the 1930s. Is that what those Republicans wanted to see happen? Was defeating Obama in 2012 so important that having the country fall into a deep depression would be worthwhile?

Obama had a stated goal of bringing about health insurance reform in an effort to bring some measure of control over the nation's ballooning health care costs. If Obama failed in that effort, health care costs – already out of control – would continue to eat up larger and larger portions of the national economy and both federal and state budgets. Is that what those politicians wanted to see happen?

In the area of national security, if the Obama administration failed, the nation could become the victim of more terrorist attacks. Americans would die and be terrorized. Is that what those politicians wanted to see happen?

In essence, what I'm suggesting is that saying you want the president to fail is tantamount to saying you want America to fail over the course of that president's term in office – i.e., at least four years. To me that is the most powerful example of "politics gone awry."

And, unfortunately, the record of House and Senate Republicans opposing virtually every legislative effort by the Obama Administration – even its efforts to get a budget passed – suggest strongly that the Republican Party as represented in Congress is doing its best to make the president fail.

The problem, of course, is that for some of our politicians, their political philosophy has taken on the aura of a religion and those people have become as much political zealots as any Christian or Muslim extremist has become a religious zealot. As a result, their minds are not open to any ideas that are at variance with their ideology just as many conservative religious people are not open to any religious interpretations that differ from their own closely held beliefs.

But closed minds do not advance the democratic process. And, as we have seen in Congress during these years of the Obama presidency, closed minds do not lead to the two political parties working together to bridge differences with workable solutions to serious problems. And, while "workable" solutions to problems might not be "perfect" solutions from the viewpoint of the left or right, they certainly would be a notable improvement over the status quo.

With that said, there is a simple explanation for why conservatives want Obama to fail. If Obama supports and gets through Congress laws reflecting policies that conservatives oppose – policies that differ from what their ideology would lead them to accept – and those laws achieve their goals, then the conservative ideological viewpoint will be proven flawed.

On a much deeper scale, that's like being told there is no Santa Claus when you are six years old. It's like being told that everything you have believed about the right way to do things is wrong. That's a tough pill to swallow for anyone. And that, I would suggest, is one reason – perhaps at a subconscious level — why so many Republicans want the Obama administration to fail.

Now, here's where common sense comes in. And I wish we could find a way to make all members of Congress (i.e., from both political parties, including liberals and conservatives) accept this: There is more than one way to skin a cat. In sports, there is more than one way to win a game. In life, there is more than one way to achieve personal goals. And in politics, there is more than one way to get things done for the country.

I realize that so far I appear to be laying blame for this state of affairs on conservative Republicans. That's only because in recent years they seem to be the ones doing the most to obstruct the work of Congress. But fairness requires this observation: Democrats had sufficient majorities in both chambers of Congress in the first two years of Obama's presidency that they probably could have passed legislation in that session of Congress, but the ideological viewpoints of a few Democrats in both houses made it impossible for Democrats to agree on their legislative goals. It was this inability of Congressional Democrats to work together more than the opposition by Congressional Republicans that prevented early passage of comprehensive health insurance reform legislation.

Members of Congress once knew how to compromise for the good of the country. They worked together. They knew each other socially and had lunch or dinner together without regard for party affiliation. And they need to get back to that way of doing things. "We the people" need them to get back to that way of doing things. Otherwise we, the people who elected them, will suffer the consequences.

One final comment: The news media is as much to blame as any other group for allowing our politics to go awry. The owners of some news outlets are blatantly using their media to advance their own political agendas. Moreover, most owners today appear far more concerned about profit than with the responsibility placed on them to serve the public interest – a responsibility placed on them by the

First Amendment to our Constitution, which ensures a free and unfettered media and protects news organizations from government interference and censorship.

Unfortunately, just when the nation's need for strong, honest news reporting is greatest, news organizations are cutting back on their news-gathering operations. I realize that newspapers and news magazines need to make enough money to support their activities. I also know that radio and television news ideally would be self-supporting. I even know that, historically, newscasts have been money-makers in the television industry. But even if the costs of maintaining viable news organizations have become larger than the revenue streams they generate through advertising, most local radio and television stations have other programming to subsidize news operations if necessary.

Moreover, most of the national broadcast and cable news outlets are owned by large corporations that also have other business interests that could subsidize – and, if necessary, should subsidize – their news departments. The owners of our news media have a responsibility to the public they serve – a responsibility to have their reporters dig out and report facts. Too often they are failing in that responsibility, allowing their reporters to merely parrot what they are told.

But short of that, here are four simple things that our news reporters should be doing at the very least: First, if politicians advance lies or half-truths, instead of repeating those lies or half-truths as if they are news, reporters should be calling them on it and pointing out the falsehoods and errors of fact. That would be news and here's the headline: "Senator Blank caught in effort to mislead voters."

Second, if politicians or political commentators make outrageous statements like wanting the president to fail, the news media – both local and national – should look hard at those statements, analyze them, and report on the implications of such statements. Imagine this headline: "Senator Blank wants the country to sink deeper into recession."

Third, when a politician lets loose with an outright lie – for example, saying that a health care proposal to pay for end-of-life counseling by physicians (something many physicians were already doing without compensation) would lead to withholding care from the elderly because it would be too expensive and then calling it a proposal for "death panels" – the news media should jump on that assertion immediately with the statement, "Senator (or whoever), that is simply not true and you know it" and pointedly correct the statement. And they should dig into the source of the proposal.

In that specific instance, the provision in the House bill to pay for end-of-life counseling was co-sponsored by at least three Republicans.[21]

This kind of reporting is not taking sides. It is, however, fulfilling the press's watchdog role by making sure the public gets accurate information instead of merely passing on misinformation and, thereby, lending credibility to political lies. As noted in the footnote, *USA Today* in this case fulfilled that obligation. Every other newspaper in the country should have done likewise with a big headline on the front page and the same story should have been featured at the top of every newscast.

Lastly, when members of Congress, state and local politicians,

---

[21] *USA Today* – August 18, 2009. "End-of-Life Counseling had bipartisan support." The article identifies Rep. Charles Boustany, R-La (a heart surgeon), Patrick Tiberi R-Ohio, and Rep. Geoff Davis, R-Ky as co-sponsors of this provision. According to the article, after Sarah Palin labeled the provision as sponsoring "death panels" and other conservatives began to echo that claim, Republican support for the provision withered.

political candidates and corporate executives fail to answer direct questions, but instead use them as described above to segue into their own key points, the interviewers should stop letting them get away with it. Wouldn't it be interesting to see an interview in which the interviewer asked the same question over and over again until either the politician answered the question or the interview came to an end? In the latter case, of course, the interviewer should point out to his listeners or viewers that the politician never did answer the question.

Of course, I'm probably tilting at windmills on this one. But I'm ever hopeful that both reporters and editors at national and local media will somehow find the courage to take back their media and do the jobs for which they have been guaranteed freedom from government interference by the First Amendment to our Constitution – in short, do a job they can be proud of. In this way, they could contribute greatly to putting our political house in order and, thereby, help this country move forward.

12 Prescription Drugs in the United States of America

Health care costs have been much in the news over the past several years. As a result, I, like many Americans, have thought a lot about this issue. One question continues to bother me: Why can people in other countries purchase prescription drugs sold by U.S. pharmaceutical companies for less money – a lot less money – than we Americans have to pay for those same drugs in our own country?

It makes no sense.

In fact, we have trade laws that prevent foreign companies from selling their products for less in the United States than they charge for them in their home countries. When they do that, we call it "dumping" and our U.S. companies can seek tariffs on the imports to offset the lower prices.

If our government won't allow other countries to "dump" their products in the United States, why is it that we allow the big drug companies to "dump" their drug products in other countries – countries as close as Canada or in Central America and the Caribbean?

I've actually had the experience of benefitting from this practice. Roughly fifteen years ago, my wife and I were in the Caribbean and needed to replenish her thyroid medicine. We paid five dollars to see a doctor and have him write a prescription for this particular brand name product (there was no generic for this particular medication) and we purchased the prescription for a very small fraction of what it had cost us through our medical insurance plan back in the United States.

At the time, I was just happy that we'd gotten a bargain. Today, I am angered by it.

What has happened to change my attitude?

First, I stopped to think about it. And, when I did, common sense told me very quickly that there is no good reason why I should have to pay more here at home for a drug developed and manufactured here in the United States than I would pay in Canada, Mexico or some Caribbean country.

Second was a belated reaction to the sweetheart deal given to the U.S. pharmaceutical industry when Congress passed the Medicare prescription drug benefit in 2003 and specifically refused to allow Medicare to negotiate prices with the drug companies. At the time, I didn't think much about it because I thought it wasn't going to affect my prescription drug plan. (See! I really am a rather typical American. If it doesn't affect me, it's not my problem!) When I think of that now, however, I am angered because it is obvious both that it does affect my Medicare prescription drug plan and that many members of Congress have sold out to the drug companies.[22] (And politicians wonder why Congress is held in such low esteem by the public.)

Third was my growing awareness of the part played in our ballooning health care costs by prescription drugs – an awareness brought about by discussion in recent years of health care costs and

---

[22] According to OpenSecrets.org, in 2002 – the election year immediately preceding passage by Congress of the Medicare prescription drug benefit – the pharmaceutical industry invested nearly $30 million in Congressional election campaigns, with 69 percent of the total going to Republican candidates. In 2008, with health insurance reform looming on the horizon, the pharmaceutical industry again invested nearly $30 million in congressional election campaigns, this time about evenly split between Republicans and Democrats.

health care reform. For information, in 2007, prescription drugs accounted for 10 percent of our $2.24 trillion national expenditures for health care.[23] In other words, we spent about *$224 billion dollars* on prescription drugs in this country in 2007.

And fourth, I learned that drug companies are now spending almost twice as much money marketing their drugs as they do in research. Moreover, as much as half or more of that marketing expense is spent on television and print advertising aimed directly at consumers for the purpose of encouraging us to ask our doctors to prescribe the drug companies' most profitable drugs, whether or not those drugs represent the most cost-effective treatment for our health problems.

When I was a medical and science writer for a daily newspaper in the late 1960s, the pharmaceutical companies justified their high prices for their brand-name drugs and their high profits by pointing to their large investment in research. They argued with some justification that, for each drug that eventually made it to market, they often spent tens of millions of dollars identifying and testing potential new drugs that did not work out for one reason or another.

This high-risk research (risky in a financial sense) was used to justify the high prices for their brand name products, which in turn were justified as being necessary to provide the income to fund the research and to provide the profits and dividends needed to attract investors.

The drug companies make the same argument today. What they don't tell us, however, is that unless they are issuing new stock specifically to obtain investment capital, their "investors" (read that

---

[23] Centers for Medicare and Medicaid Services, Office of the Actuary, National Health Statistics Group

"stockholders") are just riding the gravy train. In other words, the drug companies' high profits are not rewarding their stockholders for risking their money to fund research; they are simply rewarding them for being astute enough to purchase the companies' stock.

The push for ever-higher profits has only one purpose today – increasing the market value of their stock, which enriches stockholders, including the drug companies' executives and board members.

More importantly, they also don't tell us that their products high prices are funding billions of dollars in advertising – by some estimates, more in advertising than on research – advertising that contributes nothing to the development of new drugs.

This high level of consumer advertising is a relatively recent development.

Pfizer and Merrell-Dow started the movement to direct consumer advertising in the mid-1980s with health care ads to inform consumers about the availability of new treatments – never identifying a specific product, but encouraging people with specific problems or symptoms to see their physicians and inquire about new treatments that were available.[24]

In 1997, however, the Food and Drug Administration opened the floodgates for direct consumer advertising of prescription drugs by relaxing the rules governing such ads.

As a result, according to one study, pharmaceutical company consumer television advertising doubled in just two years from 1997 to 1999, reaching $1.9 billion. By the year 2000, fully ninety-seven

---

[24] www.enotes.com/drugs-alcohol-encyclopedia/advertising-pharmaceutical-industry 1/22/2010

prescription products had been advertised on television or in print media.[25]

This growth in direct-to-consumer advertising for prescription drugs has only continued.

Although we don't know how much any of these companies spend on marketing or on consumer advertising, a 2008 report in *Science Daily* provides a clue. This report cites a study by two York University researchers who found that in 2004, the latest year for which data was then available, U.S. pharmaceutical companies spent 24.4 percent of their sales dollars on marketing their drugs and 13.4 percent of sales dollars on research and development.[26]

In other words, for every dollar spent on research, drug companies spent $1.82 on marketing. And that's one reason our country spends so much money on health care.

For the record, I called one of the largest American pharmaceutical companies to ask about their expenditures on research and consumer advertising. I was told the information was considered proprietary and not released to the public for competitive reasons.

So where does all of this leave us? It is time to stand up to our members of Congress – both senators and representatives – and insist that the laws and/or regulations governing pharmaceuticals be changed in three ways.

First, we want the law changed to prohibit pharmaceutical companies – or any other company, for that matter – from selling products to consumers in other countries for less than they are sold in the United States.

---

[25] Ibid

[26] www.scienccedaily.com/releases/2008/01/080105140107.htm

Second, the law establishing Medicare prescription drug plans must be amended to allow Medicare or Medicare-approved prescription plans to negotiate prices with the pharmaceutical companies.

Third, if possible from a legal perspective, the tax code should be changed so that direct-to-consumer advertising is no long deductible by the drug companies as a business expense. Further, laws or regulations should be changed to require drug companies to itemize consumer advertising in their annual reports to stockholders. We need more transparency.

Finally, any law prohibiting prescription drug sales to consumers at lower prices outside of the United State should allow an exception for the sale of drug products at reduced rates to health agencies and non-governmental health organizations in underdeveloped countries so that the benefits of modern healthcare can be extended to the poorest of nations.

If members of Congress will not support, actively seek and work to enact these changes in the law or regulations as appropriate, they are admitting they have sold their votes to the pharmaceutical industry and are more interested in serving the interests of that industry than they are in serving the interests of voters in their home states and districts. We, as voters, will then know who to vote against in the next election.

13

The Politics of Climate Change
(aka "Global Warming")

The failure of partisan politics to serve the public interest is clearly demonstrated by the inability of Republicans and Democrats to find common ground for dealing with the predictions of climate change.

In fact, I often think that former Vice President Al Gore did us a disservice by his efforts to increase public awareness of the theories of global warming, the impact of greenhouse gases on global warming and the potential impact on the worldwide climate.

Why? Because his association with those theories politicized them. It wasn't his fault. It's just a fact of life and the result of the bitter partisan political structure of the United States at this time. Because Al Gore – a liberal Democrat – endorsed those theories, the gut reaction of conservative Republicans was to make a mockery of them. Had some other prominent person with no particular political association been able to publicize the theories equally effectively, the opportunity for a bipartisan approach to this issue would have been much better.

Despite the ensuing polarization, however, common sense suggests that it should still be possible to persuade our political leaders to look at this issue dispassionately by asking them to consider two simple questions:

(1) If the theory of global warming and predictions of climate change are wrong, what would be the consequences of assuming the

predictions are correct and working aggressively to reduce production of greenhouse gases worldwide?

And, (2) If the theory and predictions about global warming and climate change are correct, what would be the consequences of ignoring them as so much hokum and doing nothing about the production of greenhouse gasses?

Common sense tells me that the most sensible response to the global warming/climate change predictions can be found in the answers to those two questions. Moreover, the answers are straight-forward.

If we work aggressively to reduce greenhouse gases and the theory and predictions are wrong, we will have done the following:

- Developed large-scale sources of renewable energy.
- Developed a more efficient nationwide distribution system for electrical energy.
- Developed more energy-efficient means of ground transportation.
- Developed a wide range of new technology to support all of the above; and,
- Created exciting new areas for investment, wealth creation and employment.

On the other hand, if we assume the theory of global warming and predictions of climate change are nonsense and do little or nothing to reduce emissions of greenhouse gases, and the theory and predictions turn out to be right on the money, the consequences will include the following:

- A rise in sea level and flooding of many coastal areas.
- Changes in rainfall patterns.
- An increase in extreme weather events.

- Major loss of ecosystems and killing off of many life species.
- More severe effects longer term because of the delay in taking remedial steps.

Let's discuss these various items, looking first at the consequences of taking these predictions seriously and moving aggressively to reduce greenhouse gas emissions.

Developing large-scale sources of renewable energy: When people speak of renewable energy, usually they are thinking of wind, solar and nuclear energy to generate electricity and biofuels (principally ethanol) as a replacement for gasoline. I believe tidal energy should be right up near the top of that list.

For example, in some parts of the coastal United States, tides of six or eight feet or more are common. In the Bay of Fundy in southeastern Canada, tidal changes of 30 feet are the norm.

Historically, the approach to harnessing tidal power has been to allow the incoming tide to fill an impoundment area, close the gates at high tide, and then let the trapped water escape on the falling tide through a race to power a mill or turbine.

Today, in the search for more effective uses of tidal energy, companies are looking wherever large tidal flows are funneled through narrow waterways, creating strong tidal currents. In addition, companies are looking at the action of ocean waves as a source of energy and at narrow inland waterways with strong flowing currents as possible sources of this "hydrokinetic" energy. The problem has been finding ways to harvest that energy without disrupting natural tidal flows or otherwise harming the environment or marine ecosystems.

That problem may now be solved. The U.S. Federal Energy Regulatory Commission (FERC) in January 2012 issued its first pilot license for a tidal power project, which is now under development in New York City's East River by Verdant Power Company. By the end of 2013, FERC had either licensed, issued preliminary permits or had applications in various stages of the permitting process for a total of 28 hydrokinetic projects (see Table 7).

Table 7

Preliminary Permits Issued		14
• Tidal	9	
• Wave	2	
• Inland	3	
Preliminary Permits Pending		7
• Tidal	1	
• Wave	3	
• Inland	3	
Projects in pre-filing for license		2
• New York's East River		
• Muskeget Channel (Massachusetts)		
License Issued		1
• Reedsport OPT Wave Park (Oregon)		
Licenses Issued for Pilot Projects:		3
• Roosevelt Island Tidal Pilot (New York)		
• Cobscook Bay Tidal Pilot (Maine)		
• Whitestone Poncelet In-River Pilot (Alaska)		

Source: U. S. Department of Energy, Federal Energy Regulatory Commission

* * *

That first pilot license for a tidal power project came after Verdant Power completed a two-year demonstration project to test the world's first grid-connected array of tidal turbines. The demonstration project, which used six underwater turbines to generate 70,000 watts of power for commercial sale, has shown no discernable negative impact on the busy East River waterway, which connects Long Island Sound to New York Harbor.

At this writing, Verdant Power is in the process of building out the project in stages, with the first stage expected to be completed in 2017, when the turbines are expected to help power Cornell University's new campus on Roosevelt Island in New York City. When the project is completed, its 30 turbines are expected to produce one megawatt of commercial electricity – enough to power more than 1,000 homes. The company hopes ultimately to expand the capacity of this demonstration unit to an additional two to four megawatts of power.

A similar effort using a different turbine design is being developed in Canada's Bay of Fundy by Nova Scotia Power and its Irish partner, OpenHydro.

In this project, a 10-meter-wide "Open Centre Turbine" is planned to rest on the floor on the bay's Minas Passage and capture the tidal energy as the flow ebbs and floods. A test turbine was put in place in 2009 to measure current flows and removed in 2010. The first turbine that will be hooked up to the grid is expected to be in place in 2017. The companies engaged in this effort are members of the Fundy Ocean Research Centre for Energy (FORCE), which is constructing the station that will connect the turbines to the electrical grid.

If these and other similar projects work out, there are many places worldwide where such underwater turbines could be used to generate electricity with little negative environmental impact. One advantage of using tidal energy to generate electricity is that such energy is reliable and predictable, simplifying the challenges of feeding it into the electrical grid.

Wind turbines and solar panels, of course, also present great potential as renewable energy sources. One can already see large wind farms in some parts of the country and many more are on the drawing boards, including offshore winds farm already approved for development off the coasts of Cape Cod and Delaware. Large arrays of solar panels on the roofs of industrial buildings also are becoming more common sights. The major stumbling blocks for both of these technologies are the modernization of the electrical grid used to distribute electricity and development and/or expansion of technology to accommodate the unpredictable fluctuations in power generated by these natural sources of energy.

Biofuels – for the most part alcohol used as a substitute for gasoline – represent a different challenge. In the United States, as noted in earlier chapters, most alcohol used in gasoline is produced from corn. In general, common sense suggests it is absurd to use a major food crop to produce alcohol for fuel in a world where starvation is still a problem. I would, however, make one exception to that statement – that is, production of alcohol from sugarcane.

Sugarcane is grown widely around the world. With one major exception, most of the crop goes either into the production of sugar, molasses or rum. The one major exception is Brazil, where most sugar cane is used to produce ethanol as a fuel for automobiles and light trucks in fully integrated ethanol plants. Ethanol-powered cars and, much more common, "flex-fuel" cars and trucks – including those made by Ford and General Motors – capable of running on gasoline blends of up to 85 percent alcohol are commonplace in Brazil.

In these fully integrated plants, the residue fiber after the extraction of the sugar for production of ethanol is used as fuel in the boilers to generate electricity to power the plant. According to an analysis by the business research and consulting firm of Frost & Sullivan, Brazil's generation of electricity from sugarcane fiber residue totaled 3.0 gigawatts (GW) in 2007 and was forecast to reach 12.2 GW in 2014.[27]

My question is this: What would happen if we encouraged increased production of sugarcane in Puerto Rico (where it was once the predominant crop) and the neighboring Caribbean islands, built a fully integrated ethanol plant in Puerto Rico adjacent to the island's one existing oil refinery to facilitate the production of high-alcohol content blends of gasoline and then used that integrated ethanol plant to provide a ready market for sugarcane grown in the region?

I can foresee at least two results: One is at least a small boost to the region's island economies by providing an expanded market for a valuable crop. Another is the increased use of high alcohol-content gasoline blends with a corresponding reduction in the consumption of crude oil and gasoline. Additionally, of course, the sugarcane residue would be used to fuel boilers for the generation of electricity to power the entire operation with any excess electricity produced being fed to the local grid.

Developing a more efficient nationwide electrical distribution system: Our current system of electrical grids has been described in various news reports as "outdated," "fragile" and "barely adequate." These grids are made up of the various networks of power lines that our many electric utilities use to distribute electricity from their

---

[27] http://energy.ihs.com/News/biofuels/2008/frost-brazil-bagasse-093008/htm

generating facilities to their customers.

The fragility of the system was dramatically demonstrated in 2003 when the failure to trim trees along a power line in Ohio resulted in shorting out the system and eventually causing a blackout that left some 50 million people in the northeastern United States without electricity for many hours. The fragile nature of the system has been demonstrated many times since – as recently as the winter of 2013-14 with blackouts caused by severe winter storms.

For the future of renewable energy, the greatest challenge will be developing what is called a "smart" grid – actually a series of interconnected smart grids that will enable us to move electricity all around the country. From a practical perspective, what the smart grid will amount to is an integrated network of electrical highways with the traffic – the flow of electricity – controlled by two-way computer monitoring systems.

As with the construction of our network of interstate highways for automobiles, this nationwide smart grid will require decades to develop and cost hundreds of billions of dollars. Work is already beginning, but its completion will require support of successive Congresses and Administrations for some years to come. It will also require large scale public support because many miles of electrical transmission lines will have to be erected, meaning that many communities will have to accept new power lines running nearby.

When this smart grid is completed, we will not only be able to move electricity from one part of the country to another – something we cannot do effectively now – but the system will also be able to accommodate the variable input of power produced by such renewable sources as wind, solar and tidal energy.

So imagine this scenario: Southern California and New York City able to avoid brownouts and reduced voltages during abnormally hot weather because enough power to support the unusually high short term demand can be fed into both areas from Midwestern wind farms. Or the situation in which untrimmed trees short-out a power line as they did in 2003, but this time the slack is taken up immediately from other parts of the grid and the effects of the incident are felt only in a small, local area and that for just a few hours or less.

Or this scenario: Solar farms in the Southwest feeding the grid during the daylight hours with local fossil-fuel generating plants idling in neutral during the day, but picking up the slack as the sun starts to diminish in the afternoon and evening, until taking over completely during the night-time hours when demand on the system is at its lowest, only to reduce their output again as the sun comes up the next day and the solar farms begin once again to take on the load.

Another benefit of the smart grid will be the widespread use of smart electric meters by utility companies combined with web-based feedback to customers so that those customers can better monitor and manage their power consumption. These meters and web-based customer feedback are already being provided by utilities in a few areas.

Moreover, these smart meters can be used by utilities to enable customers who want to install solar panels or wind turbines at their homes or businesses to feed any excess electricity produced into the grid and have it credited to their accounts.

"Far-fetched," you say? Not at all. Think about it. Solar energy is generated only during daylight hours. In homes in which family members are at work and/or school during the day, consumption of electricity is often minimal. But the solar panels wouldn't know that and would provide their maximum output while consumption in the home was at its lowest. With a large enough array, it is entirely possible there would be excess electricity from the solar panels that could be fed into the grid. Similarly, commercial entities that may be closed on weekends and holidays could have their solar arrays feeding the grid on days they are closed.

Developing more energy-efficient means of ground transportation: The decision in the early 1950s by the Eisenhower Administration to develop our Interstate Highway System has had the effect of making highways our primary methods of moving people and freight. As a result, a major portion of our economy was developed around the automobile for moving people and trucks for moving freight, with the result that cars and trucks in the United States, as noted in Chapter 9, account for some 57 percent of our national consumption of crude oil.

At the same time that growth of our transportation system was being focused on cars and trucks, mass transportation was allowed to languish despite spotty efforts to provide limited high-speed passenger trains. And rail transportation of freight has been allowed to limp along, being used primarily for moving freight not economically moved by truck. Also, as noted in Chapter 9, the Intracoastal Waterway along the East Coast of the country has been allowed to shoal in many places, making its use by commercial barge traffic more difficult.

Many other countries have also developed efficient highway systems. At the same time, however, they have also developed efficient systems for moving people and freight by rail. As a result, it's possible in those countries to limit your use of the automobile to local driving and to travel longer distances easily, conveniently and inexpensively by rail – sometimes by high-speed rail. I suspect, though I don't know, that these countries have also developed efficient rail transportation systems for carrying freight.

Today, we're going to play catch-up. We have already committed to building a high-speed rail system for passenger service in some areas of the country. Hopefully, we will also improve and increase our railroad freight-carrying capacity and resume much needed dredging of the Intracoastal Waterway to encourage greater use of barge traffic for moving bulk materials.

Developing a wide range of new technologies to support all of the above: Think about some of the new technologies I have mentioned in the preceding paragraphs: computer-controlled electrical distribution systems, smart electric meters, underwater free-standing turbines for generating electricity and automobiles able to run on high-alcohol-content fuels. These are some of the new or relatively new technologies that have already been or are being developed to aid our transition to renewable energy. I cannot begin to guess what other new technologies will be developed in the next 10 or 20 years as we move farther into that world. But we can be certain of two things: (1) There will be new technologies developed to assist in this transition; and (2) the countries that lead the transition will also be the sources of those technologies and the centers of their exploitation.

Creating exciting new areas for investment, wealth creation and employment: One thing is clear: The development, introduction and expansion of new technologies provide opportunity for investment that can lead to greater national and individual wealth. It also provides many new opportunities for employment – read that "jobs." The most obvious recent example of this kind of opportunity has been the development of the Internet and the many companies that have emerged to find unique ways of exploiting and expanding upon that technology. Many of those companies did not exist before the introduction of the Internet, nor did the jobs and career opportunities they have created.

Without question, our movement toward increased use of renewable-energy sources and the development of alternative transportation systems that are much less dependent upon oil for energy will spawn similar kinds of business and investment opportunities and job creation. If we move forward aggressively in these areas in the United States, those business and investment opportunities and the jobs they spawn will be created in this country. If we do not…

Now, having said that, I must acknowledge that if all we do is focus on going "green" and pay no attention to how we manage that process, communities and regions that have depended historically on industries that would be rendered obsolete could suffer serious negative economic impact. But that doesn't have to happen. We can avoid such localized negative impacts by anticipating those problems and planning our transition to a green economy so that all regions and all communities can benefit from that transition.

Okay, so those are the potential "downsides" of assuming that the threat of global warming and climate change is real, of aggressively transitioning to renewable energy in a combined effort to reduce our dependence upon finite oil reserves and to reduce our production of greenhouse gases and then finding 10 or 20 or more years from now that it was all a false alarm.

Now let's take a more detailed look at the downsides of assuming that global warming and predictions of climate change are all a bunch of hokum and continuing to do things in the same old way.

First, a general comment: Many of the most severe effects of global warming are not predicted to occur in the United States, but the geopolitical impacts would be felt by all nations. The worst effects would likely be in Africa, Asia and the Middle East. Europe would likely also receive severe effects – possibly including much colder weather than it now enjoys, particularly if predicted changes in ocean currents were to occur. Even so, the United States would not go unaffected. And, in the discussion below, I will attempt to point out expected direct impacts on our country.

Looking at these "downsides" one at a time....

A rise in sea level: The melting of land-based glacier ice is feeding more water into the world's oceans, contributing to an increase in sea level. Additionally, as the climate warms, the average temperature of the ocean waters also is increasing, adding to the increase in sea level. Conservative estimates project an increase in sea level from seven to 23 inches by the end of this century. Those predictions do not include the impact of significant melting of the Greenland and western Antarctic ice sheets. Should that occur, the long-term increase in sea level could be as much as from 12 to 18 feet or more.[28]

An increase of as little as 4 inches in sea level would flood many South Sea islands and swamp large parts of Southeast Asia.[29] The result would be the creation of tens of millions of refugees as coastal villages gradually succumbed to higher tides. An increase of 23 inches would be even more catastrophic in those same areas.

In the United States, an increase of 23 inches – nearly two feet – would have profound effects on the East Coast from Cape Cod to southernmost Florida and the entire Gulf Coast and the adjacent low-

---

[28] Intergovernmental Panel on Climate Change (IPCC) Fourth Assessment Report

[29] IPCC report issued February 27, 2007 as reported in Global Warming Facts, national geographic .com/news, updated June 14, 2007

lying areas inland from both of those coastlines with Florida and Louisiana particularly at risk. Longer term, a rise of 12 to 18 feet would put many thousands of square miles of most U.S. coastal states under water.

Changes in rain and snowfall patterns: One result of global warming will be increased evaporation of water from the world's oceans, resulting in more water vapor rising into the atmosphere to be cooled and released as rainfall or snowfall, leading to particularly heavy rains and snow storms with more flooding of rivers and streams. Additionally, there will be changes in the distribution of rain and snow, with creation of new areas of desert in tropical areas and the creation of new forests in what are now desert areas.[30]

Actually, we may well have been given a preview of what to expect here in the United States if climate change caused by global warming is reality by the dramatically heavy snowfalls and flooding rains seen in the first months of 2010, caused in the opinion of some meteorologists by the El Nino effect. In El Nino years, warm waters in the Pacific Ocean move closer to the west coast of the Americas, bringing about changed weather patterns, including increased precipitation in some areas. With global warming, ocean temperatures are expected to rise, in effect creating permanent El Nino conditions. If indeed that happens, the flooding rains and heavy snowfalls of early 2010 could well become the norm rather than 50- or 100-year events.

The summer of 2010 may also have provided a preview of things to come in the United States and elsewhere if global warming is a reality – the hottest summer temperatures ever recorded in Russia,

---

[30] IPCC Fourth Assessment Report

including the first-ever 100-plus temperature in Moscow; record heat in the eastern United States lingering for weeks at a time; extreme rain and rain-caused flooding in Pakistan; huge wildfires caused by heat and drought in Russia;[31] and, more recently, the "polar vortex" that descended upon the United States the first week of 2014![32] All of these are consistent with the predictions of "more frequent and more intense extreme weather events due to global warming."

An Increase in extreme weather events: As noted immediately above, one result of global warming is expected to be an increase in severe weather events, including tropical cyclones, tornados, heat waves, wildfires and the incidence of extreme high tides. While there may not be an increase in the total number of tropical cyclones (hurricanes in the United States), more frequent stronger storms can be expected among those that do occur. There will also be an increase in the areas affected by drought. And, in many areas, drought leads to wildfires.

Major loss of ecosystems and killing off of many species: Climate change brought about by global warming is forecast to lead to the extinction of more than a million species as a result of disappearing and changing habitats. One highly visible habitat already suffering greatly from global warming is the Arctic ice pack, which is melting at a rapid rate with the possibility that the Arctic will experience its first ice-free summer by the year 2040. Polar bears are already suffering from the rapid loss of Arctic ice, as are the native people living in the area.[33]

---

[31] "Long hot summer of fire and floods fits predictions" by Charles J. Hanley, Associated Press, August 12, 2010

[32] "Climate Change Might be Driving the Historic Cold Snap" – http//science.time.com/2014/01/06/climate-change-driving-cold-weather

[33] Global Warming Fast Facts, National Geographic News at www.nationalgeographic.com/news updated June 14, 2007

In tropical areas, we are also seeing major losses of coral reefs as the result of the increase in seawater temperatures resulting from global warming.

Loss of Glacier Ice: In Europe, Asia and North America, glaciers have been melting at a rapid rate in recent decades. In the United States, for example, Montana's Glacier National Park has lost more than 120 glaciers since 1910, with only 127 glaciers remaining.

This loss of glacier ice has profound implications for water supplies, river flows and, in the U.S. Pacific Northwest, for hydroelectric power generation. The loss of glacier ice and the melting of the Arctic ice pack also contribute to the warming of the oceans. Ice reflects solar energy whereas water absorbs solar energy, is warmed in the process, and in turn hastens the melting of seaborne glaciers and pack ice.

More severe effects longer term because of the delay in taking remedial steps: No matter when we – all nations of the world – begin to reduce our output of greenhouse gases, it will take time to slow or stop global warming. If we wait 10 or 20 or more years to acknowledge that global warming is real and to begin reducing our production of greenhouse gases, we will not only have increased the burden of greenhouse gases during those years of delay, but will also be extending by the same 10 or 20 or more years the time before our actions can begin to take effect and global warming can be slowed, stopped and, eventually, reversed.

Again, this is simple math: For example, if we act today and it takes us (the world community) 40 years to stop the growth in our output of greenhouse gases and it takes an additional 40 years for the upward trend in global warming to level out, that's a total of 80 years. If we wait 40 years to take action, we give 40 more years for the additional impact of global warming to affect us and will still require 40 years to end the growth in our output of greenhouse gases and another 40 years (or more) to bring global warming to a standstill. In this delayed scenario, that equilibrium point is 120 years or longer in the future. (**Please note:** This example was only intended to illustrate a point – that is, the longer we wait to take action, the more severe the impact of global warming will be because of our increased time of exposure and the increased total amount of greenhouse gases produced. The time spans are given only to illustrate the point and are not intended to be scientifically accurate.)

All of this brings me back to the opening sentence of this chapter: "I have been very much surprised at the resistance of many of our political leaders to the predictions of climate change and the efforts to reduce our emissions of greenhouse gases."

It seems obvious to me that there are few if any truly serious downsides to taking action now to reduce our output of greenhouse gases even if the theory is proved wrong. To the contrary, efforts to reduce our production of greenhouse gases would bring about a large number of real benefits.

Similarly, it seems equally obvious that there are very real and serious downsides to denying the theory and doing nothing to reduce our output of greenhouse gases if theory indeed proves to be reality.

Moreover, I don't see how anyone can politicize this issue unless he is blinded by his ideological views, has his head in the sand ostrich-like, or is solely interested in feathering his own nest and has no interest in the long-term effects of his actions.

I would seriously encourage political, communications, and civic leaders of all political viewpoints to go through the same kind of risk/benefit analysis I have tried to present here. If after doing that they come to the same conclusions I have reached – and I will be surprised if people doing an honest risk/benefit analysis do not come to the same conclusions — then I would further encourage them to become part of a large and continuing campaign to educate the American public about one clear truth about climate change and global warming – that is, we just can't take the chance of assuming the theory is hokum and, therefore, of doing nothing. If we do nothing and we're wrong, the consequences will be devastating. Moreover, there is little to risk and much to gain by going green. We need to push our elected representatives in Congress and in our state legislatures into positive action on this issue.

Three more observations: First, regardless of what we in the United States ultimately decide to do on this issue, many other countries are already forging ahead to develop and adopt new technologies aimed at reducing the use of carbon-based fuels. If we decide to hunker down and hope that the theories of global warming are science fiction, we are going to be left behind on the technology curve. As a result, the new industries and new jobs that come with these technologies will be developed overseas, not in the United States.

Second, it is true that there will obviously be economic dislocations (employment losses) in different areas of the country if we move aggressively to reduce our greenhouse gas emissions, just as there have been, for example, employment losses and dislocations in brick and mortar stores and in traditional news and advertising media as a result of the Internet explosion.

BUT, exactly as has occurred with the emergence of the Internet, the overall growth in the economy and in job creation will dwarf local dislocations and job losses. Instead of sitting back and decrying potential job losses and opposing efforts to reduce greenhouse gas emissions, common sense suggests that local and state political leaders would serve their voter constituencies much more effectively by working to attract elements of these new industries and the jobs they will create so that their local communities can grow with this change rather than be left behind to stagnate.

And finally...if I were a politician in any East Coast state from Maine to Florida, any Gulf Coast state from Florida to Texas, and any Pacific Coast state including Alaska and Hawaii, I would be doing everything I could to persuade this nation to take global warming seriously. If, in fact, global warming is caused or increased significantly by human activities and if, in fact, the Greenland and western Antarctic ice sheets begin serious melting, the resulting rise in sea levels will be absolutely catastrophic for coastal areas of those states and, even, for some areas far inland. Moreover, by the time we know that melting is happening, it may well be too late to prevent disaster for many coastal areas. That's not a gamble worth taking.

14

Getting Things Done in Congress – The KISS Strategy

With the Obama Administration's effort a few years ago to push health insurance reform legislation through Congress, we had an incredibly vivid demonstration of what is perhaps the biggest barrier to bringing about major legislative change in Congress, particularly in today's highly charged partisan atmosphere: legislation becomes too big to handle.

It becomes so big and complex that few people can keep track of and/or understand everything in the legislation....so big and complex that even voters who support the legislative goal become uncomfortable with the bill under consideration. It also becomes so big that it's easy to hide pet projects....so big that it's easy for opponents to distort what the legislation would do....so big that it can contain small elements that divide the political party pushing it....so big that it makes voting against it easy....and so big that political leaders often have to make undesirable compromises to get the last few votes needed to pass it.

But there is another way to get things done – a much cleaner way to get major legislation through Congress. And that's by following what I'm calling the KISS legislative strategy.

We've all heard of the KISS principle – Keep It Simple Stupid. What I'm suggesting is that we fold that principle into a strategy for seeking complex or controversial legislative goals one step at a time.

Let me illustrate the concept with a story from my past.

When I wanted to build a vacation home many years ago but couldn't afford to hire a contractor, I decided to build the house by myself. As the cement truck drove away after I had finished pouring the footer for the foundation, I stepped back to look at the job site. A pile of sand, a stack of cement blocks and a pallet loaded with bags of cement lay nearby. And I was suddenly and absolutely overwhelmed by the task that lay before me. I can still remember that feeling more than 40 years later. What in the world made me think that I could build a house all by myself?

But as I stood there trying to wrap my mind around the task that lay ahead, I realized that I would be laying the foundation one cement block at a time and building the rest of the house one piece of wood at a time. And, as I came to understand that I would be building the house one piece at a time, the project stopped being so overwhelming. The only real challenge, I realized, would be figuring out how to put each piece in place.

It took me three years of weekends to build that house, but I got it done.

I'd like to suggest that when the president and congressional leaders want Congress to pass major legislation, they consider bringing that legislation before the Congress the same way that I built my house – one piece at a time.

I must acknowledge that this is not completely my idea. The germ of the idea came from a column written by William Greider in the magazine, *The Nation.* Although the column appeared in a liberal publication, which could be a turn-off to many conservatives, this idea applies equally to all administrations and all sessions of Congress, no matter which party is in power.

In his column, Greider wrote: "If comprehensive health care reform is out of the question, Obama Democrats can break it down into smaller pieces and try to pass worthy measures one by one." [34]

The common sense behind this idea appeals to me. I just want to take it a step farther. I would apply this strategy to as many bills as possible if for no other reason than to make it more difficult for senators and representatives to hide pork barrel projects in them. But my primary reason for urging this strategy is to make legislation easier to understand, easier to explain to the public and more difficult for its opponents to misrepresent.

Let's look at the still-much-argued health insurance reform legislation as a case in point. First, even people who supported the goals of reform were uncomfortable with the legislation because it had grown so large and complex that they could not really know what was in it.

For those who wanted to oppose it, the lengthy legislative process and the complexity of the House and Senate bills made it far too easy to arouse public anger because few citizens actually knew the legislative details or understood its provisions. It was easy to pick on little details – for example, the provision to reimburse physicians for providing end-of-life counseling – and to twist those details into something with evil intent.

How much better it would have been to pass twenty or forty, two hundred or however many single-subject bills were needed to accomplish all or most of the goals of health insurance reform – one step at a time.

Moreover, such a strategy would have forced every representative

---

[34] "Obama's Big Wake Up Call" by William Grieder. *The Nation*, January 22, 2010.

and senator to vote yes or no on each specific aspect of the proposed reform. When voting against a large, complex piece of legislation, members of Congress can justify their "No" votes on the grounds of some broad or vague objections to the bill. That would be much more difficult to do when voting on a single-subject bill – for example, one whose only content was a change in law to prevent health insurance companies from refusing to cover or to charge higher premiums for pre-existing medical conditions.

In more recent years, we have seen Congress stymied in its efforts to agree on a budget bill. Wouldn't it be interesting to see what would happen if the overall budget were broken down into a series of small bills each focused on only one specific piece of the budget, and these small bills were introduced and kept separate throughout the legislative process?

Think of it as doing a jigsaw puzzle. When you first take all of the individual puzzle pieces out of the box, they make no sense. But you have the picture of the finished puzzle on the lid of the box to guide you.

By starting with a summary of the overall budget (the picture on the lid), members of Congress would be able to see how each piece fit into the whole, and how the overall budget would compare to projected revenues. But by breaking the budget into small pieces of legislation for voting purposes, members would be forced to vote yea or nay on each specific part of the budget. It would not surprise me if many of those single-subject bills would find bipartisan support. Moreover, if some of those single-subject bills proved controversial and could not be passed, voters would know exactly where their representatives and senators stood on those specific issues.

I know that many politicians in and out of Congress will say that what I am suggesting is impossible. They will say Congress simply could not deal with the large number of bills that would be required if we exchanged the larger and more complex pieces of legislation for a large number of single-subject bills. But I disagree.

For example, we had months of hearings and debate on the health insurance reform not just because the legislation was so complex and controversial, but because its very complexity made it possible for the opposition to string out the process. Had that legislation been broken down into 100 or 200 or 1,000 single-subject bills, each just a few pages long and with each one considered separately, it could not possibly have taken any longer to bring those bills to a vote than it took to get to a final vote on the legislation that ultimately made it through the House and Senate.

I mean, how many days of committee hearings or floor debate can be justified by a piece of legislation that would do only one thing – for example, again, make it illegal for health insurance companies to deny coverage or to charge higher rates to people because they have pre-existing conditions?

Moreover, any differences between House and Senate versions of each single-subject piece of legislation would likely have been small and easily worked out in conference. Had any one of the single-subject bills contained a stumbling block in the conference committee, the blockage would have affected only that one narrow piece of legislation, not the other 999. Indeed, any truly controversial item probably would not have seen the light of day in the first place.

There are other reasons to take this approach. How often do we hear from members of Congress that legislation is so complicated and bills are so long (running to many hundreds or even thousands of pages) that members do not have the time to read them in their entirety or even know in detail what they are voting on? In fact, under the present system, most members are casting their votes on complex legislation on the basis of advice from legislative aides and lobbyists. Adopting the KISS legislative strategy would solve that problem. Members would no longer have any excuse for not knowing what each single-subject bill was all about. Media reporting on legislative proposals would also likely be more accurate, as would public understanding, simply because the legislation would be so much easier to understand. Also, politicians and talk show hosts would face a far tougher time trying to distort or misrepresent legislative proposals.

In addition, as suggested earlier, following the KISS legislative strategy offers an opportunity to reduce the number of pork barrel and other special-interest amendments that often go unnoticed under the present system until it is too late to do anything about them. It would be pretty hard to hide a "bridge to nowhere"[35] in a very short and sharply focused piece of single-subject legislation.

Of course, to make this approach work, the leadership must ensure that single-subject bills are voted up or down one bill at a time. Under no circumstances should they be bundled together into a single piece of legislation.

Finally, for purposes of illustration, let me compare how the current approach to big-bill legislation would compare to the KISS strategy in attempting to pass some of the changes in our tax laws suggested in earlier chapters.

If those proposals were lumped into a single piece of legislation,

---

[35] "Bridge to Nowhere" is a reference to a controversy that arose in 2005 when it became public that an unnoticed pork barrel project had been passed into law to provide $223 million to construct a bridge to connect Ketchikan, Alaska, with its airport on the Island of Gavina at a total cost to taxpayers of $320 million. The combined population of Ketchikan and Gavina was less than 9,000 at the time.

the likelihood of getting that legislation passed would be small. Opponents of the legislation could easily misrepresent the impact of the proposed legislation by labeling it as "a massive tax-increase bill" and repeating that characterization over and over until it became accepted by the public as truth.

Moreover, groups of people who opposed different parts of the bill could easily be mobilized into a coordinated and powerful lobbying effort – the corporate executives, Wall Street executives and wealthy taxpayers who opposed changes in the capital gains tax, restrictions on the use of tax shelters and higher tax brackets on high-income people; the food industry opponents of taxes on unhealthy high-fat content and high-sugar-content foods; and corporations opposing the suggested change in corporate tax law to require them to keep only one set of books and, therefore, to pay taxes on the earnings reported to shareholders. By mobilizing opponents to each of these provisions, it would be possible to mount major opposition to the bill.

But what would happen if each proposal was contained in its own bill and those bills were introduced, debated and voted on serially – one at a time? For example:

- A bill to tax high-fat-content foods to help defray the cost to taxpayers of obesity-related diseases.
- A bill to tax high-sugar content of prepared foods to help defray the cost to taxpayers of obesity-related diseases.
- A bill to limit long-term capital gains tax rates to stock newly issued for the purpose of raising business capital.
- A bill to limit deductions from earned income to the deductible items now allowed on Tax Schedule B – i.e., to eliminate tax shelters on earned income.

- A bill to require corporations to pay taxes on the income reported to stockholders.
- A bill to increase the marginal rate in the top tax brackets for wealthy taxpayers.

If each of these bills were to be considered separately one at a time with the next bill not even brought to committee until the previous one was acted upon and either became law or was voted down, it would be difficult to misrepresent the bill under consideration and all Americans would clearly understand what the legislation would do or not do.

In this scenario, Congress might not be able to pass all six of those bills, but they almost certainly would be able to get some of them enacted into law. And that would be an enormous improvement over having one omnibus bill shot down in flames. So here's one place in which a bit of common sense would seem to make eminent sense. It provides a practical solution to the obvious problems involved in bringing about worthwhile change in sensitive and often emotionally charged matters of policy.

Do you think we could encourage administration and congressional leaders to give the KISS legislative strategy a try? I certainly hope so. They – and, more importantly, We the People – have nothing to lose by doing so and, potentially, much to gain.

Public Education in America

15

We all know that our public schools have serious problems. Not all of our schools, of course. Every state boasts school systems that are doing outstanding jobs of educating their children. But too many schools are failing their students.

This situation, however, is not the fault of the individual schools. Or of teachers. It is a failure of our overall system of education – a system that has failed to evolve in parallel to the evolution of our society; a system that, in its way, is a victim of our dedication to democracy and our desire to give all students the same opportunity – i.e., the same educational opportunity.

But a "one-size-fits-all" system of education cannot work. Not in our complex society.

Nor can the problem be solved simply by creating a blue-ribbon panel led by corporate executives to identify changes needed to equip our graduates to fill the jobs of the 21st century. By definition, that approach will focus primarily on jobs created by new technologies and emerging industries when what is needed are ways to make our education system work for all of our students. Even worse, that kind of approach will mask the greater need by creating the illusion that something is being done to address the system's overall deficiencies.

This is a problem every citizen should care about. The future of the country will be in the hands of today's school children. Moreover, the "future of the country" is not some abstract concept. It is the future of our children, grandchildren and great grandchildren not yet born.

This situation has been building for decades and there have been many federal efforts to reverse the trend. The latest (at this writing) is the "Race to the Top," launched in 2009 to encourage states to develop pragmatic changes that will improve the effectiveness of our schools. Before that, the program was "No Child Left Behind." Both programs share the same fatal flaw: They rely on testing to measure how well schools are doing and ignore what simple common sense suggests are seven of the primary causes of our failing system of public education:

1) The failure of many parents to provide their infants and young children with an intellectually nurturing environment in their home.
2) Related to No. 1 above, the failure of many parents to participate in their children's education once they begin school.
3) The use of property taxes as the primary mechanism for funding public schools in many states.
4) Our tendency to adopt "one-size-fits-all" solutions to our public education failures.
5) Inadequate personnel management and reward systems for public school teachers.
6) Inadequate personnel management and reward systems for public school administrative and supervisory personnel. And,
7) Out-of-date secondary school education programs.

Let's look at them one at a time.

The failure of many parents to provide their infants and young children an intellectually nurturing environment in the home: One of the most basic predictors of scholastic success for any child is whether his parent(s) read to him frequently when he was an infant and young child. And while reading, whether the parent was teaching him to recognize letters and associate words with pictures. Add to that the presence of intellectually stimulating games in the home and parents who will spend time playing those games with their children.

The problem is simply described: Whatever most of us know about child-rearing, we have learned from the example that others, including most importantly our own parents, have set for us or what we may have learned in various high school or college courses. If we have not grown up with parents reading to us, or seeing other parents read to their children, the likelihood that we will read to our infants and young children is small. If we are school drop-outs, the likelihood that we will read to our children is small. And if we have children as teenagers, the likelihood that we will have the parenting skills to help our children succeed in school is small. Moreover, this lack of parenting skills as it relates to the child's intellectual development continues to affect children negatively once they enter school.

The failure of parents to participate in their children's education: Another of the most glaring differences between children who succeed in school and those who do not is the degree of parental involvement in their children's education once the child starts going to school.

I'm not talking about whether parents go to meetings with teachers or to PTA meetings. I'm talking about what parents communicate to their children about the importance of education and school, starting

– as suggested above – with reading to their very young children every day so that their children begin from the earliest years to enjoy reading.

I'm talking about whether parents sit down with their elementary-school children to help them do homework. Whether parents provide their children with both a suitable study environment (i.e., not disturbed by TV, phone calls or cell phones) and check to make sure that homework not only is completed, but is done as well as the child can do it. Whether parents are available to help with homework if needed. Whether parents make sure their children get a good night's sleep so they go to school well-rested. And, whether parents let their children know how proud they feel when their children do well at school – not that they necessarily get As on their report cards, but that they are doing their best.

These are all the kinds of things that parents of children who succeed educationally have traditionally done for their children to enable them to do well in school. First, those children know that their parents value education. They know that their parents expect them to do their best in school and that, if they don't do their best, there will be a consequence. In our family, for example, when an unacceptable report came home, the child who was not trying to do her best was grounded until the grades improved. I always found it remarkable how quickly the grades improved.

But that kind of support system is missing for many students, particularly in poorer school districts and in families where parents are "too busy" to pay much attention to their children. As a result, these students are handicapped before they put their first foot into school. And that handicap only grows with each new school year, either because their parents simply don't value education or because they don't know any better.

Teachers working in today's school systems cannot be expected to make up for those deficiencies. Moreover, no amount of testing will solve that problem. And therein lies the fundamental flaw in programs like "No Child Left Behind" and "Race to the Top."

I don't know how to solve these first two problems in the short-term. But I do have two suggestions of ways to attack the problem in the longer-term – ways that might also help some children in the nearer-term.

First, I'd like to see a "how to succeed in school" class early in the school year for all 6th or 7th grade students. This would include such things as the importance of homework, finding a good study environment free of distractions (including turning off your cell phone!), getting enough sleep, and asking for help from parents or teachers.

Next, I'd like to see a year-long parenting class as a required course for all high school students. And I'm not talking about how to feed a baby! Think about it. Where do we learn to be parents? For most of us, all we know is the example set by our own parents.

As a country, we cannot afford to continue having people become parents when they have little or no idea of how to nurture their children. And I mean "nurture" in the broadest sense. So I would like to see all high school students – boys and girls – learning how to be nurturing parents in a carefully developed, year-long course. Such a course would never encourage teen pregnancy. It would, however, fill in some of the gaps in parenting that many students experience and might well discourage teen pregnancy by helping teenagers understand the responsibility and hard work involved in effective parenting.

The class would not necessarily have to meet every day. It might meet only once or twice a week, but it would teach students how to raise their children for success. In addition to teaching the importance of reading to children, it would include learning about children's books, how to pick them out, and how they should be read to children. It should also include learning about games and play activities that will stimulate children intellectually and help them learn to think.

For school-age children, it should teach the high school students how parents can encourage their children to get the most out of school, how they can teach their children through their behavior about the importance of education, and how to provide the structure and environment needed for homework. And with all of this, it would emphasize at every opportunity the idea that the example they set as parents will provide the most powerful lessons their children receive from them – the parents.

This class should also include field trips in small groups to day-care centers where the students can put into practice some of the things they learn in class. Students who have younger brothers or sisters at home could be encouraged to practice the skills they are learning in the classroom in their own homes, perhaps keeping a diary of their activities. And, if some of those students come from homes where these parenting skills are lacking, think about the impact those students could have on their own families.

Think also about the possibility that students whose parents do not provide a suitable place to study and do homework might absorb enough of what they learn to start providing themselves with the desired study environment.

The problem with this proposal, of course, is that even though it might have a direct impact today on some students, its great potential influence is on the next generation of parents. So, what about today's families?

Again, I can't provide the proverbial magic bullet. I can, however, offer a suggestion for two places to start: First, I would offer a scaled down version of the high school parenting course to the parents of all preschool children in each school district. Moreover, if I could persuade my state legislature to fund it or, alternatively find a charitable foundation to fund it, I'd offer a financial incentive for parents to take this course – an incentive based on their attendance record that they would receive at the end of the course. Yes, I'm suggesting that we pay parents to attend these classes. That's the one way I can think of to get them to attend.

I'd also suggest offering a similar course and financial incentive to parents of children who are underperforming in elementary school. The course for these parents probably would have a somewhat different focus than the course for preschool parents, focusing not only on what they can do to help their children be successful in elementary school, but also on what they'll need to do to help their children succeed in middle school and high school as well.

Would such courses for high school students and for parents of young school-age children solve this problem – the failure of parents to participate in their children's education? I don't know. But at least it would be a direct attack on this part of the problem and it has the potential to bring about positive change. It certainly offers more hope for positive change than what we're doing now – which is nothing.

The use of property taxes as a primary mechanism for funding public schools: Perhaps the single greatest source of disparity among school systems is the reliance on property taxes as the major source of funding for public schools. It's a great system for wealthy school districts and a terrible system for poorer districts.

I am probably one of the few people in this country to stand up at a County Council meeting and ask the council to raise our property taxes if necessary to fund the school board's operating budget request for the following year – this during the 1980s when politicians were running for office on promises not to raise taxes. Needless to say, members of that county council ignored my pleas.

If lawmakers want to use property taxes as a source of revenue, that's well and good. But public school funding should come from a state's general fund and should be distributed on a per-capita basis. There should be no disparity between the funding of schools in wealthy communities and those in poorer communities unless it is to provide such special services as financial incentives for preschool parents and for parents of underperforming elementary-school students to take parenting courses.

Some people might take exception to the idea of favoring some districts with extra funds. I would suggest to those people, however, that an extra investment in those districts is analogous to practicing preventive medicine. It will save heavier public expenses in the future if it brings about a more effective education system today.

One-size-fits-all solutions to our public education failures: The "No Child Left Behind" program was what I call a one-size-fits-all solution. Just give everybody tests during the year and then require schools whose students are not scoring high enough on the tests to improve. The first fallacy of this approach is its assumption (a) that all students develop and, therefore, learn at the same rate and (b) that all students should be learning the same things. The second fallacy of this approach is that it focuses only on the symptoms of the problem and does nothing to find the causes. The "solution" too often has been for teachers to teach to the test. And even that usually brings about only marginal improvement. The third fallacy is that it causes our schools to focus on the lowest-performing students and to ignore its better students, especially its brightest students. After all, they're doing just fine.

This last fallacy was highlighted in a *Newsweek* article that included these statistics: "In the most recent global tests – scored on a 1,000- point scale – the U.S. scored a 481 in math, 497 in science and 498 in reading comprehension." These scores, the magazine reported, were either slightly below or barely above average and well behind the world's leaders, which include not only such countries as China, Japan and the Netherlands, but also includes Latvia, Slovenia and Vietnam.[36]

When parents, teachers or school administrators believe a school is failing many of its students, what I'd like to see is an independent team of educators – perhaps from a state university school of education or a specialized unit within the state superintendent of education's office – visit that school for three or four weeks to observe classes, review records and meet with students and teachers to come up with something analogous to a medical diagnosis and a custom designed program for that particular school. Notably, that evaluation and prescription might even involve actions to be taken at other schools in the district and might include providing additional funding and staff to that school.

For example, if the failing school is a middle school or high school, it's entirely possible that the basic problems at that school lie in one or more of the feeder schools. Students who come to a middle school

---

[36] http://mag.newsweek.com/2014/01/17/america-hates-gifted-kids.html

reading or doing math at a second-grade level or who come to a high school reading or doing math at a fourth-grade level cannot be expected to perform at grade level in their new school. Nor can the regular classroom teachers in those schools be expected to perform miracles with those children. In this case, the most important contribution the diagnostic team could make might be its prescriptions for improving the feeder schools. Or to broaden the offerings at the middle or high school to provide separate classes specifically geared to the students whose needs have not been met – without distracting the regular classroom teacher from the needs of students who are meeting or exceeding expectations.

In some ways, I wonder whether public schools at all levels might not be well-served by having to go through the same kind of accreditation program used by better private schools. This periodic review involves self-evaluation by the faculty of the school seeking accreditation (or reaccreditation) as well as independent outside evaluation of the school. Moreover, if schools fail to receive accreditation, they are given specific reasons for that failure and the opportunity to correct problems with the goal of finally receiving their accreditation. The advantage of such an approach is that recommendations for improvement are individualized to the specific school; many are also the result of a systematic internal evaluation by the school faculty.

Inadequate personnel management and reward systems for public school teachers: Today's public schools have inherited a flawed personnel system for teachers. In part, this heritage is a result of two facts: First, during much of our history, most teachers in elementary and secondary schools have been women; and, second, for most of our history society has not valued women's work equally with that of men.

In part, too, this heritage is a product of our reliance on local property taxes to fund education, especially when taxpayers have been asked to approve tax increases for education in referendums. It is also a product of the *public* nature of teacher pay scales versus the *private* nature of pay scales in the private sector. And, finally, all of the above led in many states to the organization of teacher unions and collective-bargaining units for teacher contracts.

What all of this has created today is the following: (1) Highly structured and rigid pay scales for teachers. (2) Relatively low salaries for public-school teachers compared to the salaries of people with equivalent educational backgrounds and years of experience in the private sector. (3) With relatively few exceptions, a situation in which outstanding teachers, good teachers and inadequate teachers all are paid from the same salary schedule. What this means in most public school systems is that if three teachers – one outstanding, one good and one inadequate – each has a bachelor's degree and ten years of experience, all will receive the same pay regardless of their differing job performance. And (4) our system makes it very difficult to weed out inadequate teachers.

Contrast this with the private sector. In my former employment, each salaried employee received an annual performance review by his immediate supervisor and was rewarded (or not) for his performance in his annual salary review. It was entirely possible for two people in the same salary-level job to be receiving widely different – as much as a 30 percent difference – paychecks.

Similarly, as a result of these performance reviews, it was possible to provide specific suggestions as to how an employee might improve his performance. It was also possible in this context to encourage underperforming employees to seek a different career opportunity or, if necessary, to set a deadline for that employee to improve his job performance or have his employment terminated. That is next to impossible to do in our public education system.

The company also offered two career tracks that enabled non-management professional employees to receive promotions to salary levels that paralleled management salary levels – a system that recognized their professional excellence without forcing them to move into management to attain those same higher salary levels.

The largest problem, of course, is that our society undervalues the work of teachers. And we justify this by pointing out that teachers really work for less than 200 days a year while everyone else works about 240 days per year. Those who make this argument go on to list all of the vacations teachers get – Thanksgiving, Christmas, spring break, and summer vacation.

What those people fail to realize, however, is that teachers need those breaks. To anyone pooh-poohing this, let me suggest that naysayer try teaching for a year – managing a classroom of from 20 to 30 children of any age for six hours a day with only a lunch break. Oh, and by the way, teaching the children at the same time. Anyone who has ever been a classroom teacher, or married to one, knows that teachers need those breaks in the school year to recharge their personal batteries before returning to the classroom. Or, maybe people who think teachers have it easy could try teaching for just one week; that would probably be long enough.

Having preached that sermon, let me address the more salient point with a question: How important is the job our teachers do compared to the job of a stockbroker, a banker, or even a nurse or doctor or engineer or salesman or attorney or any other professional you want to name?

Our classrooms teachers are molding our citizens of the future. Children often spend more time each day with their teachers than they do with their parents. Our country says we place a high value on education. Our politicians can't talk enough about the importance of education. Common sense suggests that we should place an equally high value on the people who do the actual educating. Education cannot happen without teachers.

We need to develop personnel management systems and reward systems for teachers similar to those used in the private sector. School administrators need to function more like private-sector supervisors and managers when it comes to personnel evaluations. We should also have different professional levels for teachers similar to the professional levels mentioned above so that outstanding teachers can be "promoted" to higher salary levels without having to move into administration. And, the best teachers should be able to earn salaries on a par with all but the highest-level administrators.

Finally, existing collective bargaining-units need to take a new look at their role in the system. They should be on the same side as the school boards, encouraging better personnel management systems and recognizing the need to weed out poor performers. Membership in a union or professional organization should not be a guarantee of lifetime employment as a teacher. In fact, it has been my experience that many poor performers are simply in the wrong jobs (careers), that they know their work is sub-par, and are relieved to be given the opportunity to change career paths.

But key to all of this is the development and implementation of an effective and credible performance evaluation system that all employees trust. It will take time, and it will take training for all supervisors. But no one has to reinvent the wheel. Templates for such systems already exist in the private sector. It's mostly a matter of finding the will – and political courage — to do it. With such a system in place, it would be possible to implement a multilevel professional salary schedule so that teachers can be paid something much closer to their true value to society – a development that would have the added benefit of making teaching a more appealing career choice for many of our brighter young people.

Inadequate personnel management and reward systems for administrative and supervisory personnel: The basic problem in personnel management of administrative and supervisory personnel is that too few schools and school districts have a well-organized system for evaluating administrative and supervisory personnel performance and for moving poor performers out of positions where they can hurt school or district performance.

The plain fact is that a school principal can make all the difference in the world in how well teachers are able to teach. For example, a school principal who worries about how it will look on his or her record if "too many" students are sent to alternative schools – and who, therefore, allows disruptive students to remain in the regular classroom – can make it almost impossible for teachers in those classrooms to teach. More importantly, it is unfair to other students because the disruptive students are truly disrupting the learning environment.

District administrators who are loath to support discipline-oriented principals or to remove principals who are "soft" on discipline are equally culpable. In a very real sense, the atmosphere in any school is established by the principal. But the atmosphere in a school district is set by the district superintendent and his administrators.

What our school systems need is the same kind of annual performance review system for their administrators that is prevalent in the best large corporations – the same kind of performance review system recommended above for teachers. In such a system, each person in the hierarchy is given a performance review by his immediate superior and his performance is evaluated against established criteria – criteria that relate to how well the person is doing his job, not to test scores. Moreover, those performance reviews are in turn reviewed by higher administrators so that there is a check on the system.

Salary increases are determined by the performance review. Perhaps more importantly, performance reviews can also provide the basis for recommending advancement to a position of greater responsibility or, alternatively for moving someone to a different job for which he may be better-suited, or for termination. But everyone in the system knows how the performance evaluation system works and, as the organization gains experience with it, people come to trust the system.

There should also be several salary levels for each of the various supervisory and administrative positions so that outstanding personnel can be rewarded for their outstanding performance without having to be promoted to a higher position to receive a higher salary.

Out-of-date secondary-school educational programs: When I went to school, most of the standard junior and senior high school courses involved English, history, social studies, science, math and foreign language. We also had shop for boys and home economics for girls, plus music and art. These courses assumed students would be going to college. We also had vocational high schools for students who had no interest in college but who wanted to pursue a trade.

Those course offerings were fine at the time. There really were, by comparison with today, a rather limited number of career opportunities for men or women. But as technology has changed, and as society has changed, career opportunities for our youth have become so many and so varied that it boggles the mind. And yet we continue to require students to take three or four years of math, including algebra and geometry, four years of English (mostly literature), three years of science and four years of history/social studies – all of this to gain a high school diploma.

While the traditional course of study is entirely appropriate for students who will go on to college, it is equally inappropriate for many if not most of the students who will not be going to college.

In the 21st century, we need a jobs, life skills, and career-oriented secondary education system. First, we must acknowledge that not everyone can or should go to college. Secondly, we must start valuing college and the alternatives to college equally. Thirdly, for students who do not aspire to college, we must make school relevant to them, their lives and their aspirations.

And there – in that last point – is what common sense suggests is at the heart of our problem: Making education meaningful to the many students who find school boring and who are now failing or dropping out because, as far as they are concerned, school is irrelevant to their lives.

One reason these youngsters find school irrelevant is that they have no idea what they want to do with their lives. In part – perhaps to a very large degree – this is because no one has ever shown them any options beyond what they see in their daily lives.

So what I want to do – what I believe our secondary schools should do – is to develop a comprehensive, two-year survey course beginning in seventh grade to open students' eyes to the multitude of job and career opportunities available to them. In short, this survey course would be designed to expand all students' horizons. It should include jobs and career opportunities open to the complete spectrum of student capabilities, from the most limited to the most intellectually challenging.

As part of this survey course, young adults already working in as many of these areas as possible should be brought into the classroom to talk to students about their jobs, the pay scale, the long-term opportunities and what they – the students – will need to know to succeed in those jobs. It should also include field trips for small groups of students so they can actually see people working in real life. And, because the opportunities in any local area represent only a fraction of the world of opportunities that exist, the U.S. Department of Education should contract professional video companies to develop a series of half-hour video programs to introduce students to as complete a presentation as possible of the broad spectrum of job and career opportunities to supplement what schools are able to do in their local areas through field trips and classroom visits by local workers.

This two-year program should be designed so that as many students as possible enter the ninth grade with personal education goals leading to any of the several jobs and/or career paths each student finds appealing. We should not expect any student to seize upon any one career and be locked into that career path, but should instead allow students to choose several different possibilities if they want to do so.

Second, our high schools should develop four-year career-path education programs tailored to those many career choices so that as students decide what jobs/careers interest them, they can see how school is relevant to their choices. In a sense, many schools do some of this already by working with local industries to develop curricula to prepare students for the jobs those businesses offer. The difference in what I am suggesting is that schools would be developing curricula that relate also to their students' interests and that expose each student to several different job or career paths.

Third, when students express interest in possible job or career paths, guidance counselors should sit those students down and review with them exactly how the school will help them prepare for their first jobs in those areas. Moreover, such counseling should be a yearly exercise so that students can see how their classes and, therefore, school itself are relevant to them. Ideally too, students could choose (within reason) their courses for the following year, much as college students can select their courses from a list of required and elective courses. Giving students the opportunity to choose courses (even though some are required) could go a long way toward giving them ownership of their schooling.

And fourth, this system must be flexible. Students must be able to shift their focus as they move through school and their interests change, or their horizons are expanded. Students must not be locked into a particular pathway in ninth grade. They must always have – and know that they have – different options available.

The problem, of course, is that our public schools are set up for mass education based on a predetermined classical curriculum that was set in stone one hundred or more years ago. But do all high school graduates really need three years of our present-day science courses? Or to study Shakespeare? I think not. The fact is that our present high school curriculum is outdated and based on societal expectations and professional opportunities that are unrealistic or, frankly, no longer exist for most people.

What I'm suggesting is tailoring public education to the needs of students. And, for students not aspiring to college, tailoring our math and science courses to both their career choices and to everyday living (the simple math needed for managing a checkbook, comparison shopping, using credit cards, saving money and the power of compound interest, for example) so that they can see how what they are learning will be helpful. It is a different and much more difficult approach to education. It would certainly pose challenges for many of our secondary- school teachers, who would have to spend summers expanding and adapting their subject matter to fit into more varied career-oriented curricula. But if that is what is needed to keep most of our young people interested in school, giving them hope for the future, and providing them with the tools needed to become productive and contributing members of society, then we have no choice if we want our schools to be successful.

Finally, as some more progressive school systems already are doing, we need to forge a better partnership between our schools and local employers so that all students interested in career paths available locally have the opportunity to participate in work/study programs. Moreover, through modifications in state law (education is a state function, after all) employers should receive some kind of tax incentive to participate in such programs.

Now, I know that my suggestions are much more complex than I am making them sound here. Collectively, however, they serve as a different way to look at our public schools. Our traditional way of looking at them is not working for a large segment of our student population. That is very costly for society. Our students do not have to read Shakespeare to become contributing members of society. With rare exception, however, they do have to complete high school.

So those are my seven areas of suggestion. Will they solve all of our problems? Almost certainly not. But rather than more slogan-rich programs like "No Child Left Behind" or "Race to the Top," we need real change in the way we run our public schools. The suggestions I've offered are an attempt to point the way to such meaningful and worthwhile change.

Religion Gone Awry 16

The following message was posted on a sign outside a small church in rural South Carolina:

"Some minds are like concrete –
thoroughly mixed up and permanently set."

This chapter came to me as an unexpected surprise. It was not on the list of subjects I made while planning this book. In fact, I awoke very early one morning with my mind churning and was unable to go back to sleep. By the time winter daylight began peeking through the window, I had written this chapter in my head, even going over it mentally and changing parts of it in my mind to bring it to completion. And, when I got out of bed, I headed straight for my computer.

Given that the subject is religion, some might ascribe my early-morning awakening and inspiration to divine revelation. But I think not. I think instead that ideas I have been thinking about for years both consciously and subconsciously finally and suddenly emerged as a coherent whole, possibly triggered by my completing the chapter "Politics Gone Awry" less than 10 hours before my early-morning awakening.

I think it was the notion of something "gone awry" that coalesced all of these thoughts – thoughts I was not even aware were moving around in my head. And I think that happened because the phrase "gone awry" describes almost perfectly what I believe has happened to some religions in this world.

The kinds of things related to religion that have been bothering me over the past dozen or so years are:

- The notion that people can achieve salvation and be welcomed by God to Paradise because they are willing to fly an airplane full of innocent people into a building filled with innocent people, or to strap explosives around their bodies and go into a crowded wedding reception, or into a bus, or into any other crowd of people and blow themselves up for the purpose of killing and wounding as many people as possible – all in God's name.
- The belief that the only way to Salvation is through Jesus Christ and that any person, no matter how good that person's life has been, who has heard of Jesus Christ but has not accepted Him as his Lord and Savior will not go to heaven, but instead is condemned to eternal hell and damnation.
- The inability of Christian fundamentalists (probably also Islamist and other religious fundamentalists, though I have had no direct exposure to them) to accept that some of their beliefs may be wrong even when confronted by fact. For example, the belief that our world is only a few thousand years old when carbon dating proves otherwise, or the rejection of evolution when we can actually see evolution taking place in viruses and bacteria even within the space of months or a few years.

Those are the kinds of questions I've been wrestling with. But the question I woke up with in the wee hours of that morning is this:

If one starts with the belief that there is a God and that God is indeed the creator, how do we reconcile a God who would create such diversity in our world – diversity of minerals and rocks, of elements, and of plant and animal life, diversity of weather, of environments and ecosystems, and diversity among humans in their skin color, their languages, their cultures and their beliefs – how do we reconcile that God with the notion of a God who would tolerate only one faith and only one way of acknowledging Him and worshipping Him?

I cannot reconcile that contradiction.

Instead, a metaphor my sister offered me some years ago makes a much better fit with a belief in God the Creator.

She said, "Think of God as being at the top of a mountain. There are many pathways up that mountain. And each of the world's different faiths is represented by one of those pathways."

That strikes me as a good, common-sense way of looking at religious diversity.

But we live in a world of religious conflict caused by religious fundamentalists who are convinced that theirs is the one true religion. And, as I lay there in my bed, I asked myself: What is the difference between Islamic fundamentalists and Christian fundamentalists?

But when I asked that question and tried for what seemed like hours to answer it, I finally realized that it was the wrong question. The question that needed asking was: What is the ***similarity*** between Islamic and Christian fundamentalists?

The answer that jumped out at me as I lay there unsuccessfully trying to go back to sleep is this: Both Islamic and Christian fundamentalists are absolutely convinced that they are doing God's work – that theirs in the one True Cause.

Osama bin Laden believed he was doing God's work in waging

war against the "unbelievers," attempting to bring down America (the "Great Satan"), and spreading Islam, the one true religion, to the world.

At the same time, Christian fundamentalists believe that Christianity is the one true religion, that they are directed by God to spread Christianity throughout the world and that people like Osama bin Laden and anyone else opposed to their efforts to bring Christianity to the heathen are doing Satan's work.

But let's face it. They can't both be right. Moreover, there is no way to determine with certainty which religious belief might be right. And, any claim that one or the other is truly doing God's work will be based solely upon belief.

But what if neither of them is right? What if neither one is doing God's work?

If, as many people believe, there is now and has been throughout time a constant conflict between good and evil – in the eyes of many, good embodied by God and evil embodied by Satan – then is it not possible that both Islamic and Christian fundamentalists have been blinded by their zeal, tricked into doing evil and are bringing only increasing destruction and conflict to the world?

When I considered that question, I knew I had to add this chapter to my book. I have answered the question for myself. It is the only answer that makes any sense to me. But it is a question that each person must answer for him or herself.

If the answer we come to collectively is one dictated by faith that one or the other of these religious militants is indeed doing God work, then I can only say, God help us all because we are doomed to religious conflict and its horrors for the rest of our existence.

If, however, we come to the conclusion that neither group is in fact doing God's work, but instead represents a perversion of religion, then perhaps we can work together to bring sanity out of chaos and create a world that revels in all of its diversity – including its religious diversity.

Finally, I would like to share a quotation from a novel I was given as a Christmas present. It was not a novel I would ordinarily have read. But insofar as I am writing these words, perhaps there is a reason I was given this book. In any case, the character speaking these words is an Iranian woman.

"There is a serious problem with people who think they are doing God's work," she said bitterly. "Once moral ambiguity is eliminated, every human equation evaluates to infinity. Without moral ambiguity, people become capable of anything – any arrogance, any conceit, any gross stupidity….Any crime, any atrocity…."[37]

To that, I can only say, "Amen."

---

[37] *The Disciple* by Stephen Coonts. St. Martin's Press. 2009 – Page 205

Firearms in the United States

17

"A well regulated militia, being necessary to the security of a free state, the right of the people to keep and bear Arms, shall not be infringed."

The quotation above is taken from the Bill of Rights and is the complete text of the Second Amendment to the Constitution of the United States.

This Amendment has been interpreted throughout my lifetime as guaranteeing citizens of the United States the right to own and carry firearms.

I would like to offer a different interpretation, one which I believe the U.S. Supreme Court could adopt if the justices had the courage to do so.

It is important, I believe, to focus on the reason given in the text of the Second Amendment itself for the existence of this amendment. "A well regulated militia, being necessary to the security of a free state..."

First, some history: When the Bill of Rights was written and adopted more than 200 years ago, there was deep concern that a too-strong federal government with control of a large standing army might trample upon the rights of states and of their citizens. For this reason, the founders of our country placed limits on the power of the federal government to raise armies. State militias, they believed, would be adequate to provide for the defense of the country – militias controlled by the states, not by the federal government. It was this set of circumstances that led to the Second Amendment quoted above.

The Constitution gave the federal government the power to raise an army, but the strong feeling against the notion of there being a standing army kept the federal army small throughout the 19th century – for practical purposes, until World War I.

Today, the militias of the early years have morphed into the National Guard units of the various states. Moreover, the world situation, modern warfare and a comfort with our system of government have resulted in the existence of a large standing U.S. military.

In the late 18th century and through most of the 19th century, members of militias had to provide their own firearms. In the 20th and now the 21st century, the government provides firearms for our modern day militias – the National Guard – and for our federal Armed Forces.

From a practical viewpoint, what that change means is that it is no longer necessary for citizens to purchase firearms to serve in our modern militias. All they have to do is to sign up, and the "militia" – the National Guard – will provide them with any necessary firearms.

But somehow we have developed the mindset that the Constitution gives people the right to own firearms – guns. This has been interpreted to mean that almost anyone can purchase whatever kind of firearm he or she wishes – including military style weapons – to have as his or her personal firearms. And, that any one person can own as many of them as he or she wishes.

The result is that there are an estimated 270 to 310 *million* firearms in the hands of private citizens in this country – roughly enough for one firearm for every man, woman and child. Ironically, those firearms apparently are owned by only 37 percent of the people – an average of almost three firearms per gun owner.[38]

In part, this belief that the Constitution guarantees the rights of citizens to own guns stems from the process by which the United States was developed. The country expanded from the original coastal colonies westward into wild lands where firearms were a key to survival – not only for self-defense, but also for hunting (securing food). We developed an entire culture around the western man with his six shooter and Winchester rifle.

But those days are long gone. Guns are not necessary in today's world to secure food. For the most part, they are not necessary for self-defense. In fact, were it not for the spread of firearms throughout our society, there would be no need for anyone to have a gun for self-defense.

Our misinterpretation of the Second Amendment has led us into catastrophe. We suffer a mass killing – which the FBI defines as four or more people being killed – by someone using a gun every two weeks on average. In the seven years from the beginning of 2006 to the end of 2012, there were 175 mass killings involving the use of a firearm in this country. These killings took place in 40 states and claimed 898 lives, not counting the shooters. Only Hawaii, Alaska, New Hampshire, Vermont, Rhode Island, Delaware, Mississippi, South Dakota, Montana and Idaho were spared these horrors.[39]

Worse, more than 47 percent – almost half — of the mass killing

---

[38] http://www.pewresearch.org/fact-tank/2013/06/04/a-minority-of-americans-own-guns-but-...

[39] USA Today

were family killings.

And these numbers do not even include the killings involving only one, two or three victims. During the eight years from 2003 through 2010 – again, the most recent time span for which I was able to find data – we had an average of almost 11,000 homicides per year in this country[40] – most of them involving the use of firearms. That is an average of 30 homicides – murder by gunfire – every day!

And even closer to our homes and families, an average of *20 children and teenagers are hospitalized for gun injuries every day* in our country and six percent of those young people die as a result of their gun injuries.[41]

The events that made me decide to write this chapter occurred in the first weeks of 2014: On Jan. 13, in Roswell, New Mexico, a 12-year-old boy carrying a band-instrument bag walked into his school gym where students were awaiting the first bell. He pulled a shotgun out of the bag and shot two other students – an 11-year-old boy and a 13-year-old girl. Fortunately, no one was killed. But the two students were seriously injured.

Four days later, two 15-year-old students – a boy and a girl — were wounded by another student in a shooting in a high school gymnasium in Philadelphia. And three days after that, a 23-year-old teaching assistant at Purdue University shot and killed a 21-year-old senior student.

It's time to wake up people!

We are the most murderous people among the developed countries

---

[40] This average number was calculated from data in a statistical summary provided by the United Nations Office on Drugs and Crime. http://www.unodc.org/unodc/en/data-and-analysis/homicide.html

[41] USA Today, January 27, 2014, reporting on a study in the February, 2014, issue of the medical journal, *Pediatrics.*

in the world (Table 8). And it is all because a powerful lobbying group – The National Rifle Association – has ensured that people who will support their view of the gun control issue are elected to Congress and because our elected officials and our courts have been cowed by gun advocates and pro-gun lobbies.

The Second Amendment does not guarantee the right of any citizen to go out and purchase a gun. It does not prohibit state or federal governments from passing laws limiting the sale or ownership of firearms.

What the Second Amendment does do is guarantee citizens the right to join their state militias – the National Guard – or the Regular Armed Forces and, in doing so, to bear arms in the defense of their country.

It is time for the federal judiciary up to and including the U.S. Supreme Court to face up to this fact.

And, if our courts do not have the courage to face this fact, we will have to elect a Congress that will strike down the Second Amendment and state legislators who will ratify that change in the Bill of Rights. This one specific issue, I submit, argues powerfully for public funding of elections of members of Congress as discussed in Chapter 2 (An Independent Congress) so that we can have a Congress that is not owned by the National Rifle Association or any other special interest group.

Even when we finally are able to limit the sale of guns in this country, it will be many decades before the millions of guns now in the hands of citizens can be taken out of circulation. But if we can enact effective gun-control laws to prohibit the sale of all firearms and ammunition except those that can be used legally for hunting wild game, and if we can provide attractive incentives for people to turn in firearms of any kind, eventually we will have a chance to bring this terrible epidemic under some semblance of control.

If nothing is done to curb the spread of firearms – and, indeed, even if something is done to curb their sale – here is something to think about: Harkening back to my earlier discussion of the concentration of wealth in our country, the disappearance of our middle class, and the growing gap between the "haves" and the "have nots" in these United States of America, I fear that we may indeed already be arming the "militias" who will form the core of violent opposition to the continuation of present trends in our country today. If that happens, it will indeed be bloody.

Table 8
Gun Ownership and Firearm-related Deaths in Developed Countries

Country	Guns per 100 people	Firearm-related Deaths per 100,000 people
United States	88.8	10.2
Switzerland	45.7	3.84
Finland	45.3	3.64
Sweden	31.6	1.4
Norway	31.3	1.78
France	31.2	3
Canada	30.8	2.44
Austria	30.4	2.94
Germany	30.3	1.3
New Zealand	22.6	2.66
Greece	22.5	1.5
Belgium	17.2	2.43

Luxembourg	15.3	1.81
Australia	15	1.04
Denmark	12	1.45
Italy	11.9	1.28
Spain	10.4	0.63
Portugal	8.5	1.77
United Kingdom	6.2	0.25
Netherlands	3.9	0.46
Japan	0.6	0.06

Source: http://abcnews.go.com/blogs/health/medical-unit/ ABC News, Sept. 19. 2013 by Sydney Lupkin. "U.S. Has More Guns – and Gun Deaths – Than Any Other (Developed) Country, Study Finds."

Final Thoughts 18

What are these "final thoughts?" They are narrow subjects which, by themselves, do not require separate chapters, but which I wanted to address. Hence, this chapter. And, my final thoughts.

Final Thought No. 1: "Congress as a Lifetime Career"

The view and, indeed, the hope of most members of Congress seems to be that their service in Congress should be a lifetime career. That's not the way it was meant to be. The idea that a U.S. senator would serve more than 47 years and remain in office until he was 100 years old as did Sen. Strom Thurmond of South Carolina makes a mockery of our system. And when Sen. Robert Byrd of West Virginia died at age 92, he had served even longer than Sen. Thurmond – nearly 52 years.

With all respect to both of those men, we need younger people in Congress – people who have the energy, vigor and stamina to work actively at their jobs 40 or 50 or even 60 hours a week rather than relying almost entirely on staff members to do their work for them.

We also need younger people who are in touch with the real world outside of the Washington Beltway rather than politicians who have spent so much time in Washington that they are, in fact, out of touch with that world. Going back to their districts or to home states to "meet with constituents" – read that, their political supporters and/or campaign donors – does not constitute being in touch with the real world. Nor does hosting one or two town hall meetings every year. You need to have been *living in* and *working in* the real world in the relatively recent past to know and understand the world of everyday people.

We need term limits – plain and simple. Whether those limits should be two or three terms for senators and five or six terms for representatives, I do not know. But to keep Congress functioning as it is supposed to function – representing the *public* interest – and to get fresh thinking and fresh ideas we need more turnover than we get today.

When I raised this question some thirty years ago while attending a professional seminar in Washington to learn more about the functioning of government, congressional staffs told me the problem with term limits is that it would break up the "continuity" of the membership. With term limits, they said, members of Congress would have to depend on their staff to provide continuity from one session of Congress to another.

My polite reply is this: Baloney!

Term limits do not means that all or even most of the Senate and House seats would be changed at the same time. It just means that members could not make a career out of being a congressman or senator. Term limits would also limit the amount of power an individual senator or congressman could amass. In short, the same logic that led to enactment of term limits for the president of the United States applies to members of Congress.

The problem, of course, is that any amendment to the Constitution must originate in Congress and few present members of Congress would vote voluntarily to limit their congressional careers. They like their jobs too much. And they like the "three Ps" that go with that job – Prestige, Power and Perks.

The challenge, therefore, is for "We the people" to find a way to create a large enough grass-roots groundswell to make our senators and representatives understand that we – the people who elected them – want this change to our Constitution. And then, if we cannot persuade our existing lawmakers to create reasonable (i.e. relatively short) congressional term limits, then we need to start supporting candidates who will take a public oath to support such an amendment before they are elected. And once we get that amendment out of Congress, we will need to press our state legislatures to ratify it. Not an easy task. But a task well worth undertaking.

Final Thought No. 2: The News Media

I touched upon the role of the news media in Chapter 11, but feel strongly enough about this subject that I want to expand upon those comments.

For many years, we have been told and I have believed that the press is, in effect, a fourth branch of our domestic government. In fact, it is called "The Fourth Estate." In that role, the news media, protected by the First Amendment to the Constitution, was intended to be one of the most powerful components of our system for keeping government honest.

Today, for the most part, our news media have either been castrated or bought.

First, the media have been intimidated over the past 30 or more years by constant and repeated attacks on the "liberal" media. As a result, too many newspapers and broadcast-news organizations have essentially abandoned their role of keeping politicians honest. Oh yes, they are quick to jump on adultery. Or on charges of ethical misconduct, criminal activity or blatant hypocrisy. But by and large, our news media allow politicians to say whatever they want to say without challenge and simply regurgitate those political statements to the public.

Moreover, both newspapers and broadcast media are cutting their news staffs and either sensationalizing news to attract readers, listeners and viewers or becoming so bland as to offend no one. Broadcast-news outlets – radio and television news – are more concerned about ratings than they are about content. Oh sure, with their self-promotional slogans, they talk a good game. But most of it is smoke and mirrors produced by public relations or advertising agencies, not substance.

Secondly, major media outlets have been purchased by wealthy individuals or companies controlled by wealthy individuals who are using those outlets to advance their personal political agendas. When I write that the media has been "bought," what I am saying is that these owners are hiring "news" people who either agree with their owners' political views or are willing to mouth those political views in exchange for their high salaries.

Some would argue – with justification – that the news media traditionally have been more liberal than conservative. This was probably because the nature of a reporter's job was to expose him to many of the less pleasant aspects of our society. Having said that, I was trained and grew up in the tradition of reporters recognizing their own biases and bending over backwards to keep those biases out of their reporting. I would suggest that that attitude appears to be the exception today rather than the rule.

Regardless, the single most important ingredient the press can bring to news coverage about our government and politics is to question what they are being told. Expressed another way, the most important single ingredient the news media can bring to news coverage about our government is a healthy dose of skepticism.

In fact, any reporter worth his paycheck is skeptical. After the revelations about untrue or misleading statements by our government leading up to and following the invasion of Iraq, many news organizations did *mea culpas* about their failure to question what they were told.

They acknowledged that instead of questioning what they were being told, they merely reported it. But it was more than that. In merely reporting what they were told, they lent credibility to those statements and thus aided and abetted our government in its efforts to mislead us, the public, into supporting the invasion of Iraq.

Since then, some reporters, trying to show they have learned their lesson, have been standing up at news conferences with the president asking questions that challenge the veracity of his statements. But those reporters and their news organizations have missed the point.

Their jobs are to question ***every*** politician's position and statements, not merely to focus on presidential press conferences. When Senator Smith, Representative Jones or candidate Brown steps in front of a microphone and makes a statement about the issue of the day, any news organization that merely puts that piece of videotape on its newscast or reports that statement in its news pages is only serving as an unfiltered conduit for political statements.

We don't need the news media for that.

We need the news media to look at those statements critically and, if there are inaccuracies or distortions in them, to expose those errors and challenge the Senator Smiths, the Representative Joneses, and the candidate Browns of the world to validate what they are saying in an effort to get at the truth.

And there is the key phrase: "...to get at the truth."

As noted in an earlier chapter, the Nazi propagandists Goebbels made frequent use of "the Big Lie" during the 1930s and World War II. Essentially, the idea is that if you tell a big lie, and then repeat it over and over, eventually people will accept the lie as "truth."

I submit that we have seen the emergence of the "Big Lie" technique of propaganda in the past ten or twenty years by politicians and political organizations in their efforts to arouse public opinion against their political opponents or against legislative efforts of their political opponents.

I further submit that the news media, instead of exposing the "Big Lie" when it raises its ugly head, are merely passing it along as if it were truth, thereby lending it credibility. Certainly in the lead-up to the Iraq invasion, the press made the Bush Administration's "Big Lie" work.

The guarantee of freedom of the press in the First Amendment – "Congress shall make no law...abridging the freedom...of the press" – is more than a license for news media to print or say whatever they want to print or say. Those words in the First Amendment place on the media a heavy responsibility – and that is a responsibility to keep our government and our elected officials, including members of Congress, honest.

That responsibility requires hard work, not laziness. It requires informed skepticism, not blind acceptance. It requires reporters and editors who seek knowledge and truth, not ratings, and it requires reporters and editors who are unafraid of offending people in positions of political power by holding them to the truth.

We're not getting much of that today. For the most part, what we're getting is a press that is being used by politicians for their own narrow political purposes. In fact, as I suggested in Chapter 10, politicians coached by skilled public relations professionals are playing the media like so many musical instruments to produce whatever melody the politicians want the public to hear. Moreover, reporters and editors are letting them get away with it.

As a result, for practical purposes, instead of playing its role as the guardian of our democracy and of our democratic process and values, the Fourth Estate has become a toothless and almost worthless paper tiger.

It's time for that to change.

Final Thought No. 3: Income Taxes

Income-tax time is approaching as I write this and, in the past few weeks, I have heard a number of people complaining about taxes. Also, while writing about taxes in Chapters 5 and 6, it occurred to me that too many people – perhaps, even, most people – seldom if ever stop to think about what their taxes are buying for them. They think only about "government" taking their money.

Common sense suggests that it's about time our government started telling us what we're buying with our tax dollars. To that end, I suggest that every individual taxpayer receive a thank you letter from The White House each year after filing his or her tax return. Accompanying that thank you letter, there should be a small, easily read and understood brochure showing broadly speaking how tax dollars are being used in that year's budget and what percentage of the budget is consumed by each of those uses. It might also show changes from the previous year's budget.

The booklet should also include a quickly understood chart showing where the government's income comes from – the percentage of income from different income levels of taxpayers, from small corporations, from large corporations and from special-purpose taxes so that each taxpayer can see how he or she fits into the whole.

Finally, as suggested briefly earlier, our income taxes should be recast to represent a "governmental fee for service," with the amount of the fee based upon the taxpayer's income. The logic of this suggestion is this: The more a person benefits from our system of government and the social, legal and economic framework and environment provided by government, the higher the governmental fee for service he should pay. Insofar as a person's income is a direct measure of how much that person has benefitted from living and working in this entity called The United States of America, it is appropriate for government to base its service fee upon that person's income. The same logic applies to corporate taxes.

If all this were done, perhaps more taxpayers would come to understand what they are getting for their money. They'd know how their tax dollars fit into the system. They would see plainly where the biggest chunks of our tax dollars are spent. And who knows? It's possible that some people might even begin to feel better about paying their taxes…I mean, their "service fees."

Final Thought No. 4: Our Country at a Crossroads

As I noted at the very beginning of this book, Thomas Paine in his historically famous pamphlet *Common Sense* urged the American colonies to declare their independence *"while they were small enough to be united in their goals."*

Was he prescient? Has our country become so large, so diverse with so many competing interests that we have become too large to be united in our goals?

Our country today is at a crossroads. In our first 200 years, we grew from a collection of colonies seeking independence into what, during most of the 20th century, was arguably the most powerful nation in the world, both militarily and economically. The question before us is this: What will we become in this the 21st century?

Will we continue the trend of the last 30 to 40 years as a nation divided by political ideology and increasingly dominated by powerful special interests and, as a result, so unbalance the three-legged stool that represents our American social, economic and political structure that it topples over? Or will the American people – the "We the people of the United States…" cited in the Preamble to our Constitution – find a way to come together to restore the needed balance among the three legs of our national stool, restoring national stability so that we can continue to grow in a manner that makes all of us once again feel good about our country and proud to be Americans?

About the Author

John Roberts is a former general assignment reporter, education writer and medical and science writer for a daily newspaper. He subsequently entered the world of corporate public relations, where his initial duties included writing for the employee magazine and writing technical and analytical articles for the company's external magazines.

As he progressed through his public relations career, Roberts managed the corporate press office, participated in training of corporate executives for television interviews, managed the public relations services for major businesses and wrote speeches for corporate executives.

In subsequent years, Roberts also worked extensively as a freelance writer, including writing newsletters and press releases for a conservative public interest group and interviewing scientists and political leaders for articles he was commissioned to write.

His great non-professional interest throughout his life has been sailing and, in the late 1970s, he began writing articles for *Yachting* and, subsequently, *SAIL* magazines. Since that time he has written as author or co-author six books related to boating.

In *Uncommon Sense*, Roberts has brought his professional and personal experience – beginning with his covering the Republican and Democratic National Conventions in 1964 when he was a summer editor of the University of Iowa's *Daily Iowan* – to bear on a series of issues important to the nation. He has attempted to make this book nonpartisan in the belief that common sense is not a partisan concept. His interest is in discussion for the purpose of developing pragmatic solutions to problems, not ideology.

In fact, Roberts believes that both liberals and conservatives too often are so convinced of their own rectitude – of the correctness of certain long-held, so-called "core principles" – that they have lost the ability even to consider the possibility that other ideas may offer better approaches to solving problems in the world in which we now live. What is needed in politics today, Roberts argues, is thought and discussion, not slogans and talking points.

This book – *Uncommon Sense – A View from the Middle* – is an attempt to stimulate that thought and discussion.

Roberts holds a bachelor of arts degree in English from Columbia University in New York City, a master's degree in journalism from the University of Iowa, and was a science writing fellow at Columbia University's Graduate School of Journalism. Although he continued with his writing career, Roberts retired from the corporate world at the end of 1988 to go sailing.

www.ingramcontent.com/pod-product-compliance
Lightning Source LLC
Chambersburg PA
CBHW072126270326
41931CB00010B/1682
9780990796404